How to Do Apologetics
by P

"Knowing how to explain and defend the Catholic Faith, especially to those who are hostile, is something every Catholic should be ready to do. Patrick Madrid's new book explains in simple, straightforward language the art and science of apologetics. This book is a must-read for any Catholic who takes his or her Faith seriously and wants to be prepared to share that Faith with others."

— Most Rev. Michael J. Sheridan, Bishop of Colorado Springs

"If I need a doctor, I search for the best in the field. If I look for advice on apologetics, I do the same. Patrick Madrid has done it again with *How to Do Apologetics*. Loaded with practical advice and overflowing with resources, this book is a must for the new army of Catholics ready to face the culture with the full force of Catholic and biblical truth. Madrid has been doing this longer than almost anyone, and now you can take advantage of all his decades of success."

— Steve Ray, author of *Crossing the Tiber*

"As an apologist, I am often asked not just the 'what' when it comes to giving reasons why we believe what we believe as Catholics, but I am also asked the all-important question of *how* to do the work of communicating those answers. In *How to Do Apologetics*, Patrick Madrid masterfully provides the one-stop shop for answering that question. This is an exceptional presentation of rock-solid theological and philosophical information coupled with the indispensable logical and rhetorical tools that will empower all who read it to be able to effectively communicate the fullness of the Gospel message, which we alone as Catholics possess, to any and all who inquire. Definitely a must-read for any Catholic who loves the Faith, from new convert to seasoned apologist."

— Tim Staples, Director of Apologetics and Evangelization,
Catholic Answers

"What distinguishes this book on apologetics and makes it truly indispensable is that its author, one of the most well-known Catholic apologists of our time, explains in an easy, conversational style not merely what the arguments are, but how to actually use them. This is a practical guide, filled with illustrations of real-life apologetics encounters Patrick Madrid has had over the years. It's as enjoyable to read as it is immensely helpful."

— Kenneth Hensley, coauthor of *The Godless Delusion*, professor of Scripture at St. John's Seminary, Camarillo, California

HOW TO DO APOLOGETICS
Making the Case for Our Faith

HOW TO DO
APOLOGETICS

Making the Case
for Our Faith

PATRICK MADRID

www.osv.com
Our Sunday Visitor Publishing Division
Our Sunday Visitor, Inc.
Huntington, Indiana 46750

Nihil Obstat:
Msgr. Michael Heintz, Ph.D.
Censor Librorum

Imprimatur:
✠ Kevin C. Rhoades
Bishop of Fort Wayne-South Bend
September 21, 2015

The *Nihil Obstat* and *Imprimatur* are declarations that a work is free from doctrinal or moral error. It is not implied that those who have granted the *Nihil Obstat* and *Imprimatur* agree with the contents, opinions, or statements expressed.

Our Sunday Visitor Publishing Division, Our Sunday Visitor, Inc., 200 Noll Plaza, Huntington, IN 46750; 1-800-348-2440

ISBN: 978-1-61278-583-7 (Inventory No. T1279)
eISBN: 978-1-61278-388-8
LCCN: 2016930323

Cover design: Amanda Falk
Cover art: Shutterstock

PRINTED IN THE UNITED STATES OF AMERICA

CONTENTS

A select list of recommended book, video, and audio resources for students of apologetics, arranged by topic, appears on page 167.

Introduction

I got started in apologetics about thirty years ago. There was nothing then even remotely resembling the robust and widespread apologetics movement that now exists in the United States. Back then, before apologetics had become "cool" in certain circles, there were no contemporary Catholic apologetics books to be had, no audio resources, no apologetics magazines, conferences, or training programs. There was no Catholic radio to speak of then, and the fledgling Catholic network EWTN featured virtually no apologetics programming. Of course, being the pre-Internet era, there were also no apologetics websites, YouTube videos, or apps. About all an Anglophone student of apologetics had available to learn from in those days were the relatively few apologetics books from decades earlier — important works by men such as Fr. Arnold Lunn, Fr. Ronald Knox, G.K. Chesterton, Frank Sheed, and Archbishop Fulton Sheen. One particular apologetics gold mine that helped me immensely was the classic three-volume tour-de-force, *Radio Replies*, by Frs. Leslie Rumble and Charles M. Carty, originally published in 1942. The fact that it is still in print and still selling steadily, seventy-five years later, is testimony to the power and clarity of the answers these two priest apologists brought to the table in their efforts to defend the Faith against challenges raised mainly by Protestant skeptics and atheist critics of the Church. More to the point, *Radio Replies*' remarkable longevity attests to the profound and very often irresistible potency of the truth when it is presented cogently and plainly.

I feel most fortunate to have embarked on what became my life-long love for and exploration of the world of apologetics at a time when apologetics materials were scarce and few people bothered with it. It made the exploration that much more of an adventure for me — exhilarating, at times — when something I read, whether from a modern or very early apologist, turned into a key that opened doors leading to new and unexplored aspects of Catholic doctrine, praxis, and history. Learning both the mechanics and the content of apologetics was for me, in those earlier days, immensely satisfying. The more I learned, the more I realized how vastly more I had yet to learn. And it was contagious. Along the way of this exploration, I met men who would become lifetime friends and colleagues, many of whom have made prodigious contributions in this field. Maybe *we* will be the "Rumbles" and "Cartys" for future generations.

As the years wore on, the American apologetics movement began to come into its own. At first, in the late 1980s, "defending the Faith" was regarded by not a few priests and bishops as retrograde, antiecumenical and (worst of all!) "pre-Vatican II." After all, this suspicion of apologetics had been drummed into American seminarians by professors who, in the 1960s and 1970s, saw that project as hopelessly at odds with the new "spirit of Vatican II" and all the dubious notions that *that* stood for. In one sense, they were right about that. Authentic apologetics, one that seeks to clearly and convincingly present the truths of the Faith in a way that is conducive to conversion, is antithetical to a wishy-washy, insipid Catholicism. But as time went on, those of us who were actively involved in the Catholic apologetics movement (Karl Keating, Scott Hahn, Peter Kreeft, Tim Staples, Mark Brumley, Jesse Romero, Steve Ray, Fr. Mitch Pacwa, Fr. Ray Ryland, and several other key figures I was privileged to have as colleagues and fellow workers in that particular corner of the Lord's vineyard) began to see the sudden, rapid rise and proliferation of apologetics resources — a veritable explosion of tracts, magazines, books, tapes (then CDs, then digital downloads), conferences, and eventually websites, and so on — all in just the past thirty years. It was truly amazing and very gratifying to go from essentially nothing to where things stand today. (Thank you, Lord!)

And now, thirty years later, as I find myself riding if not exactly *into* the sunset, at least off in that general direction, and as more and more young, new apologists are taking their places in the vineyard, I thought that it would be right and just for me to offer a modest synopsis of many of the things I have learned along the way. This book is my attempt to crystalize as best I can what I've come to see as the broader outline of apologetics as such — its structure, components, and primary methodologies — at least as I've experienced them. I'm eager to acknowledge with gratitude that everything I learned as an apologist I learned from countless greater minds and nobler souls than mine. As a fledgling "defender of the Faith," sitting at the feet of the true masters of apologetics — the Fathers, the medieval doctors, the Counter-Reformation apologists, and all those who explained and defended the Catholic Faith in each subsequent generation down to my own, I truly came to understand the meaning of the old adage, that the only reason we can see as far as we do is because we sit on the shoulders of giants.

To borrow a line from St. Paul, perhaps the most preeminent Christian apologist ever, "For I have received from them that which also I deliver unto you" (cf. 1 Corinthians 11:23).

My hope in writing this book is to pass along to you something of that great patrimony I have received. To convey it in my own words as shaped by my own experiences in endeavoring to put it into practice for the glory of God and the salvation of souls.

CHAPTER I

What Is Apologetics and Why Is It Important?

The most riveting scene in the movie *A Few Good Men* unfolds when a tenacious prosecuting attorney grills Colonel Nathan R. Jessup (played by Jack Nicholson) about his alleged role in a murder. The relentless cross-examination inexorably forces Jessup closer and closer to admitting something he is trying to conceal. Eventually, the prosecutor shouts, "I want the truth!" Jessup cracks under the strain and bellows, "You can't *handle* the truth!" and then admits his guilt.

That message, whispered cajolingly — "You can't handle the truth" — is the subtle, imperceptible subtext of much that modern culture insists is important: mindless entertainment, our mass addiction to gadgets and games, feckless pursuit of pleasure and distraction, surfeiting our bodily appetites for sex, drink, and food. None of these are truth. Worse yet, our tendency to immerse ourselves in futile, worldly amusements prevents us from ever really grappling with the Big Questions of life, such as: "Why am I here?" "What is the purpose of my life?" and "What happens to me when I die?" As Socrates famously declared, "The unexamined life is not worth living for a human being." How sad that so many people never take the time to examine the things that really matter, stretching forth their minds and hearts toward the truth, toward God. Apologetics is a practical way of using logic and facts to help others lift their eyes from base, inconsequential distractions and gaze upward to contemplate the truth in all its beauty.

Apologetics accomplishes this task by offering those who will listen rational explanations and defense of the truth, the highest and most important of all including the truths that God exists, He loves you, He wants you to be happy, in Jesus Christ He took a human nature to save us from our sins, He died on the cross for our salvation, He promises forgiveness to all who will accept it. He established a Church replete with many treasures, all for us: the Holy Eucharist and the sacraments, the Holy Bible, Apostolic Tradition, and so much more. All of these truths are worth defending because they are life-giving and beautiful. Without knowing them at least to some extent, no human being can be truly free or completely happy.

Truth is the intellect's most precious possession. It is to the mind what accurate navigational coordinates are to an airline pilot or what a physician's correct diagnosis is to the patient. A pilot who navigates according to faulty coordinates will not reach his intended destination. A patient who receives an erroneous diagnosis of the pain in his abdomen could very well die if the wrong course of treatment (or no treatment at all) were prescribed. Truth enables us to avoid errors and to arrive at correct conclusions. Knowing and living according to the truth is always important, even in small things, while in serious matters, such as engineering a suspension bridge or calculating how much fuel to load into an airliner flying from Los Angeles to Sydney, the lack of truth can be catastrophic.

Common sense and our own personal experiences tell us that a mind imbued with truth is clearer, broader, brighter, and more vigorous than one in which the truth is not present. *That* mind, by comparison, is dark, cramped, shallow, and sluggish.

Your mind is designed for knowing truth just as your body is designed for drinking water. The purer and more abundant the water, the healthier your body will be. When water is scarce or dirty, the body gets sick. But while the body can imbibe too much water, the mind can never have too much truth. The human mind is limited, yet it nevertheless has an infinite capacity for truth because God, who is truth personified, is infinite. We must know and embrace truth and be ordered toward it just as the needle on a compass points toward true north, which it will do so long as the compass is free from interference or damage.

Try to imagine how unpleasant and dangerous this world would be if no one cared about truth for its own sake. If no one made an effort to push past mere human opinions and preferences and strive to know the truth about such things as mathematics, physics, biology, and chemistry, the world would be a very dangerous place indeed. For example, how could you know whether a bridge is safe enough to drive your car over the one hundred foot deep gorge that it spans? If the engineer who designed that bridge did not know the absolute truth about the math and physics of bridge-building but, instead, based his calculations solely on his own private opinions and preferences, chances are, his handiwork wouldn't last very long, nor would those who happened to be driving their cars over it one time too many.

Now try to imagine a world in which mathematicians, engineers, physicists, biologists, and the rest *did* care about and strive for knowing the truth about things but there was no external, objective means for any of them to ever really know if he or she had actually *found* the truth.

In this world, there are no standards against which one's individual efforts to ascertain the truth could be tested, no way for their conclusions to be verified or disproved, no recourse to an external standard by which calculations, working hypotheses, and theories could be tested and vindicated or disqualified. It's obvious why no one would want to live in that world either. It's hardly better than the first.

Now, the third scenario is not hypothetical. It's the real world in which we find ourselves today. In every scientific discipline, ascertaining the truth about things and valuing truth for its own sake is not simply highly prized but is absolutely demanded, and thus, rigorously and relentlessly pursued across the board. The empirical method has become the primary means of testing the reliability and accuracy of claims by comparing and contrasting them with empirical data. This enables scientists, mathematicians, and so on, to avoid conclusions based on bias rather than objectively verifiable data.[1] We can thank God that we actually live in *this* world. In the world of science, mathematics, accounting, et cetera, discovering and adhering to objective standards of truth are not just important but are rightly regarded as absolutely necessary.

Okay. We all understand that truth is important in math, science, et cetera. No one argues with this. But for some strange reason, many people today seem to take a very unscientific approach to matters of faith and religion. And in my own search for answers to the question, "Why be Catholic?," I determined early on that merely having a good feeling about the Catholic Church is no substitute for knowing whether or not the teachings of the Catholic Church are true. For me, plausibility is not enough. I need to know whether these teachings are, in fact, the truth. Because if they aren't, I decided, I want no part of the Catholic

Church. In fact, if Catholic teaching is false, or if even *some* Catholic teachings are false, then, I told myself, I'd hit the door running and never look back.

Over the years, I've been challenged by countless Protestants, Jehovah's Witnesses, and Mormons with biblical and historical arguments against various truths. Other challenges came from Muslims, Jews, Hindus, and other non-Christians, not to mention atheists. Each in his own way and with his own set of objections, challenged my Catholic beliefs using, variously, the Bible, historical events, logical arguments, claims to revelations that were incompatible with the claims of Jesus Christ, science, and the dull yet forceful cudgel of denying God's existence. More than a few atheists have over the years taken their fair share of whacks at my belief in God, though with about the same effect as one who attacks a piñata with a feather duster.

As a youth, passing through a gauntlet of arguments Bible-believing critics have used trying to convince me that the Catholic Church is not Christian, I always knew, in the back of my mind, that eventually I would encounter more sophisticated and formidable arguments against the Catholic Church. But when newer and more formidable arguments against Catholic teaching popped up, something fascinating happened each and every time.

I'm talking about how the objective standards of truth I turned to (whether historical, biblical, or logical) always seemed to vindicate the Catholic teaching under question. I say "seemed" in that even if it didn't seem vindicated in the eyes of the Protestant or the atheist with whom I was discussing matters, I became convinced that the other guy's argument just didn't hold water.

Some arguments in defense of the Catholic Church can be tested empirically, others cannot. But this is not a problem because not all evidence needs be scientific to be valid and legitimate. Unlike mathematical or material things, such as atoms, azimuths, and animals, I am not suggesting that theological propositions — such as the existence of God or the Real Presence of Christ in the Eucharist — can be proven scientifically. While there are objective, empirical methods for measuring, verifying, and even *dis*proving theological claims, they cannot be positively proven with mathematical certitude the way, for example, it can be proved that the radius of a circle is equal to pi times its radius squared.

The goal of this book is not so much to *prove* the truth of Catholic teaching but to show how, using biblical, historical, and logical proofs, one can demonstrate confidently and effectively that Catholic teaching is reasonable, consistent, and compelling. The old saying is true, "You can lead a horse to water, but you can't make him drink." Which is why, in this book, I will teach you how to "salt the oats" so that the horse will *want* to drink the water.

Catholic philosopher Peter Kreeft explains what steps one must take in assessing any truth claim, whether scientific or religious, if the one making the assessment wants to be logically consistent and truly open to the facts.[2] Regarding the question "Can you prove life after death?" Kreeft says:

> Whenever we argue about whether a thing can be proved, we should distinguish five different questions about that thing:
>
> > 1. Does it really exist or not? "To be or not to be, that is the question."
> >
> > 2. If it does exist, do we know that it exists? A thing can obviously exist without our knowing it.

3. If we know that it exists, can we be certain of this knowledge? Our knowledge might be true but uncertain; it might be "right opinion."

4. If it is certain, is there a logical proof, a demonstration of why we have a right to be certain? There may be some certainties that are not logically demonstrable (e.g., my own existence, or the law of noncontradiction).

5. If there is a proof, is it a scientific one in the modern sense of "scientific"? Is it publicly verifiable by formal logic and/ or empirical observation? There may be other valid kinds of proof besides proofs by the scientific method.

Kreeft continues:

The fifth point is especially important when asking whether you can prove life after death. I think it depends on what kinds of proof you will accept. It cannot be proved like a theorem in Euclidean geometry; nor can it be observed, like a virus. For the existence of life after death is not on the one hand a logical tautology: its contradiction does not entail a contradiction, as a Euclidean theorem does. On the other hand, it cannot be empirically proved or disproved (at least before death) simply because by definition all experience before death is experience of life before death, not life after death.

"If life after death cannot be proved scientifically, is it then intellectually irresponsible to accept it?"

Only if you assume that it is intellectually irresponsible to accept anything that cannot be proved scientifically. But that premise is self-contradictory (and therefore intellectually irresponsible)!

You cannot scientifically prove that the only acceptable proofs are scientific proofs.

You cannot prove logically or empirically that only logical or empirical proofs are acceptable as proofs.

You cannot prove it logically because its contradiction does not entail a contradiction, and you cannot prove it empirically because neither a proof nor the criterion of acceptability are empirical entities.

Thus scientism (the premise that only scientific proofs count as proofs) is not scientific; it is a dogma of faith, a religion.

When assessing the truth claims of the Catholic Church, scientifically verifiable evidence is important and helpful, but it is not the only kind of evidence to consider. John Henry Newman, for example, arrived at his conclusion that "to become deep in history is to cease to be Protestant," in part because of the power of the objective historical data he analyzed. But it also involved his willingness to draw the necessary conclusions toward which the data points.

For example, as early as the year A.D. 90, Pope Clement issued directives to the members of the church at Corinth on how they were to resolve certain vexing controversies that roiled that Christian community. In breathtakingly direct language, he asserted his authority over their affairs in a way that one could only expect would have provoked indignation from the Corinthians unless his authority were not recognized by them.[3]

"Hey, Clement," one can just imagine the Corinthian leaders retorting, "mind your own business! You take care of your church and we'll take care of ours." But they did no such thing. In fact, for generations the Church in Corinth revered Pope Clement's letter, regarding it as inspired Scripture and including it among the books of the New Testament read during the Divine Liturgy.

Many examples of Catholic teaching, including the papacy, the Eucharist, the sacraments, honoring Mary and the saints, the existence of purgatory, the Mass as a sacrifice, and infant baptism were clearly present in the early Church. My book *Why Is That in Tradition?* details much of the evidence for these claims. The facts of history, for example, as well as the objective data found in the Bible, are important empirical streams of evidence in the work of apologetics. They assist us in the process of validating or invalidating various theological claims. But those bodies of evidence are really only useful to apologetics when used in discussion and debate between those who already believe in the trustworthiness of the Bible; for example, Jews, in the case of what Christians call the "Old Testament," and Christians, in the case of the Old and New Testaments. Atheists and non-Christian believers in God, however, do not place any stock in what the Bible says.

Discussion between Christians and atheists involves what is known as "natural apologetics," an approach in which the Christian seeks to demonstrate the reasonableness of theism solely on logical, rational grounds (that is, without any appeal to anything like "divine revelation," which atheists reject in any case).

Apologetics geared for non-Christian theists, such as Hindus, Jews, Muslims, and Buddhists, requires what's known as "Christian apologetics," in which the common-ground belief that God exists (regardless of how "God" may be understood in any given religion) becomes the foundation upon which the Christian can build the case for the claim that Jesus Christ is truly God incarnate. This is done by demonstrating the ample rational and historical evidence that corroborates this claim.

My experience of encountering objections to Catholic teachings, listening closely to the objection, testing the objection, and drawing a conclusion as to whether or not it was correct usually happened informally, in discussions with non-Catholics, non-Christians, and nontheists. Sometimes these interactions went on long enough to afford me ample time to really dig into the evidence, pro and con, and finally make a determination based on a fair amount of careful study of the facts. Examples of this kind of thing would include long-term apologetics discussions with non-Catholic friends who, over weeks and even months, kept up a sustained effort to dissuade me from being Catholic. Other times, the time frame was more compressed but still significant. One particularly vivid memory of this kind of encounter sticks out in my mind.

CHAPTER 2

A Case Study in Apologetics Conversations

Years ago, I had to catch an early morning flight out of Orange County's John Wayne Airport. Stepping into the first-class cabin,[4] I was pleased to see that it was largely empty, so I'd likely be able to have plenty of room with no one seated next to me. I glanced at my boarding pass to see what my assigned seat was, and was dismayed that the window seat next to mine was already occupied by a stern-looking Middle Eastern man in his mid-forties. Not knowing if other passengers would arrive just in time to fill up the other seats, I plopped down in my assigned seat with the intention of moving to another seat as soon as the flight was ready to depart.

"Hey, once everyone's boarded, I'm going to move to another seat so we'll both have more room," I told the man next to me. I figured he'd appreciate the extra elbow room if I moved.

"Oh," he said, unsmilingly. "Does this mean you do not want to sit next to me? Is it because I am a *Muslim*?"

I was embarrassed that he would suggest such a thing and, I must admit, also chagrined because I *had*, in fact, felt a mild pang of anxiety when I noticed he was Middle-Eastern.

"Of course not!" I said, not wanting to offend him. "I just figured you'd want extra room." I realized then that, like it or not, I'd be sitting next to this guy even if the rest of the seats were wide open. After no more than two or three minutes of obligatory *small* talk he got down to business. I'll call him Khalid.

"I am a Muslim," Khalid said matter-of-factly, searching my face to gauge my reaction. "I believe that there is no God but Allah, and Mohammed is his prophet. What about you? Do you believe in God?"

Suddenly, I was very happy with my assigned seat. If nothing else, I knew this would be an interesting flight. Man, was I right about that.

"Oh yes. I believe in God!" I smiled broadly. "I'm Catholic and believe in Jesus Christ, the Son of God, the Messiah and Savior of the World."

"Allah does not have a 'son'!" he parried emphatically. "Jesus, peace be upon him, was a great prophet, but he was *not* God. In fact, he was a Muslim."

"*Right on!*" I thought to myself as I mentally rubbed my hands together in anticipation, "this is going to be a *really* good flight."

For the next several hours, Khalid and I had a lively but friendly discussion about Christianity and Islam. He wasted no time getting down to his appeal to me to become a Muslim. I told him I would be happy to listen to any and all reasons he wanted to give to support his beliefs under one condition: When he had said his peace, he must agree to listen with an open mind to my reasons for believing in Jesus Christ. Both of us followed through on this promise. After about an hour of his giving me an uninterrupted series of arguments intended to convince me that Islam is the only true religion, it was my turn.

I spoke first about my personal faith in Jesus, how I had come to believe that he is indeed God, not *a* god or a godlike being, but God incarnate. It was necessary to explain before all else that Christianity is not, as Muslims mistakenly think, "polytheistic." The Father, Son, and Holy Spirit are not three gods, they are not separate beings, as Khalid was convinced Christians believe. I did my best to explain the Catholic doctrine of the Trinity, that there is One God in Three Persons. This is a profoundly mysterious yet still, to some extent, knowable truth. God, I explained to Khalid, is pure spirit. He is eternal, all-powerful, all-knowing, all good, all holy, utterly transcendent (i.e., outside of space and time and therefore immaterial), and is *personal*, not some kind of amorphous "force" à la *Star Wars*. So far, so good. Khalid agreed with all of these beliefs.

"Now," I pressed further, "because God is infinite, that means there can be no barrier, no limit to his knowledge and his love. The same is true of his freedom and his power." Everything in the universe, every *thing*, is finite, no matter how large it may be. The only thing that exists that is infinite is God himself. So, while God knows every thing in the universe perfectly, because each thing is finite, at a certain point it "runs out," and therefore there is a finite limit to what can be known about it. But God's knowledge is *infinite*, I explained. Khalid agreed with this.

I proceeded to say that the only way God's knowledge could be infinite would be if there were some infinite thing, something that itself had no limits, that he could know infinitely. The only thing that God can know infinitely, I said, is himself. From all eternity, God has known himself. His self-knowledge, in fact, is similar to the image of yourself you see reflected in a mirror. That image of you in the mirror is an exact reflection of you, but it is not you. However, with God, the image of himself, his self-knowledge, *his word* about himself, cannot be separate from him or else there would be a second "infinite" thing. No, this infinite self-knowledge is in fact not something separate from God himself. It is his Word, a person, the very image and reflection of the Father. Christians know him as the eternal, unbegotten Son of God.[5] The Father and the Son know each other perfectly, infinitely, equally, and eternally. This must be so, or else there would be some sort of division or hierarchy in God. And they also know each other perfectly, infinitely, equally, and eternally. This infinite mutual love between the Father and the Son is also a Person, the Holy Spirit. Thus, I explained to Khalid, the Catholic Church, far from teaching that there are three Gods, teaches rather that there is only One God, there is only one divine substance or nature, and that it is shared equally by the three persons in the Trinity.

I wasn't able to spend anywhere near as much time as I would have liked explaining this key concept to Khalid, but at least, when I had finished with this part of my apologia for Christianity, he admitted that he now had an idea of what Christians mean by the Trinity. Before our discussion, he admitted, he thought Christianity was simply a polytheistic religion that just talked about "one God" but didn't really mean it.

Next came my explanation that, as it says in the Gospel of John, chapter 1, verse 14, "The word of God became flesh and dwelt among us." Jesus Christ is the incarnate Son of God, not in the sense that God produces offspring the way human fathers do, but in the sense that the eternally begotten Son took flesh for our salvation. I spoke about how humanity had become stranded in sin and alienation because of Adam and Eve's original sin.

God in his mercy freely willed to save us from this disastrous predicament. And because we human beings are powerless to save ourselves, he became one of us; he came very near to us, in the Incarnation of Jesus Christ to save us from our sins.

For this reason, I explained, Christ's three-year public ministry of preaching the Good News of salvation, casting out demons, performing miraculous healings, and raising the dead, was followed by his arrest, torture, and crucifixion. And after his body had lain for three days in the tomb, he rose again from the dead, just as he promised he would.

It took the better part of an hour to explain carefully all of the above as I spiraled in toward the central point I wanted to make to Khalid: Jesus Christ is God, sent to redeem and save us by his atoning death on the cross. We are all sinners in need of God's mercy and grace, and the way to receive that is to obey God's commandment "that we should believe in the name of his son Jesus Christ and love one another" (1 John 3:23). In other words, I told him, Jesus is *your* savior, and you need to become Christian to accept his free offer of salvation.

Khalid's reaction was about what I had expected. He brushed aside my claims saying that Islam is the true religion and that I must become Muslim. I wasn't the least bit bothered that he hadn't been persuaded by my explanations. I know that for some people, such as Muslims, it can be extremely difficult to break out of the preconceived biases and misconceptions people have given them about Christians and Christianity. I told Khalid I'd be happy to send him some follow-up materials to help him study the issue further.

By the time our flight was on its final approach to our destination, Khalid and I had each done our best, given the time available, to lay out our respective cases for our beliefs. It was obvious to me that he was not persuaded by my case for Christ, but I could see that he at least understood that case more clearly. For his part, he wrote down a few Muslim-apologetics websites he suggested I explore. When the plane landed, we shook hands, exchanged business cards, and agreed to stay in touch and continue our conversation via e-mail.

Over the next few weeks, I made good on my promise and watched a few of the Islamic apologetics videos Khalid had recommended. I studied the arguments closely, checking a few claims here and there, and made every effort to allow the best possible arguments for Islam and against Christianity to have a fair hearing.

Some of the arguments the speaker offered were clearly fallacious and easily refuted; others were more sophisticated and required an effort on my part to research the facts. But in the final analysis, after subjecting my Catholic belief in the Trinity and in Christ as my Savior to as rigorous a challenge as the Muslim apologist could muster, I came away not only unconvinced that Islam is the true religion, but also more convinced than ever that the message of Jesus Christ is not only true but eminently defensible. I could say with perfect honesty that yet another series of challenges to my faith in Jesus Christ and my Christian beliefs had been decisively answered and reinforced for me.

I was a bit disappointed, though not really surprised, that although Khalid quickly answered my first follow-up e-mail asking what I thought of the Muslim videos, he did not respond subsequently to the books, DVDs, and website links I sent him. Once he knew that the Muslim videos had not persuaded me to become Muslim, he never responded again. I can only hope that something in the materials I sent him and in the testimony of my Christian faith will at some point have a positive effect on him. Who knows? Perhaps someday he will come to faith in Jesus and become Christian. Perhaps I will one day meet him in heaven where we'll have an eternity to discuss the truth.

Conversations such as that one have been an important part of my life as a Catholic, especially early on, as I sought to test the truth claims of the Catholic Church. I wanted to find any flaws, ferret out the untruths, and face up to whatever facts might disprove the Catholic Church's teaching. Although I have encountered much undeniable evidence of the deplorable things that some Catholics have done, I could not uncover anything that could actually refute Catholic teaching.

I have found that the more one grapples with the biblical, historical, and logical facts involved in Catholic doctrines the more difficult it becomes to explain away the evidence. And the more likely it is that that person, if he's open to the evidence, will be persuaded by it and will, in due time, become Catholic.

As I have seen with my own eyes and felt with my heart and mind, Catholic truth has an irresistible gravitational pull. Countless converts to the Catholic Church have told me as much over the past twenty-five years. Though journeys taken by these converts vary widely, it seems they all have one thing in common: to their surprise, the very things they once were certain are false — the Catholic Church and its teachings — turned out to be true.

John Henry Newman again comes to mind as an example of a man once so dead-set convinced that Catholicism was of the devil that he preached sermons about the pope being the Antichrist. Eventually, however, as he investigated the evidence in favor of Catholic teaching, he revised his opinion of the Church so dramatically that he embraced the Faith he had once reviled. And he spent the remainder of his life explaining and defending it to those who, like he himself once had, attacked the Church and its teachings without really understanding them.

I've seen it happen many times before. Take, for example, the hardcore, committed Protestant folks who attended a public Catholic/Protestant debate and wound up converting to the Catholic Church afterward.[6] One former Calvinist woman I know told me that she attended a 1995 debate I did with two Calvinists and a Lutheran expecting to see the Catholic Church get "stomped on" (her words). She even brought a carload of her Catholic friends to the debate in hopes that they would "see the light" and abandon the Catholic Church in favor of Protestantism. I marveled as she explained what happened: She declared that she had never heard the Catholic response to the standard Protestant arguments against the Catholic faith. And she had never before heard the Catholic *critique* of the Protestant principles of *sola Scriptura* (i.e., Scripture alone) and *sola fide* ([justification] by faith alone). The debate shook her up so much that she felt compelled to start investigating the Catholic Church. Within the year, she had converted and was received into the Church. From time to time, she sends me a note or an e-mail letting me know how she had given a CD set of that debate to a Protestant acquaintance who then decided to convert.

I must hasten to point out that such debate-related conversions, when they happen, are surely realized *in spite* of my many flaws and failures as a debater. But conversions often do follow in the wake of public debates. I believe this happens because the truth of the Catholic Faith is powerful and attractive. It has its own powerful gravitational pull. Whether the issue at hand is the Real Presence of Christ in the Eucharist, the existence of God, the divinity and Resurrection of Christ, the communion of saints, or the Catholic teaching on Scripture and Tradition, whatever it may be, these truths are beautiful and coherent, not always easy to comprehend but always attractive, sometimes alarmingly so, when viewed for the first time in the full light of reason.

This is why apologetics is important. It is the perennially necessary task of clearing away whatever obstacles might prevent someone from laying claim to the truth, something all have a right to because God created us to know the truth as fully as humanly possible.

> *"If you continue in my word, you are truly my disciples, and you will know the truth, and the truth will make you free"* (John 8:31–32).

CHAPTER 3

Tools of the Trade
Logic, Arguments, and Evidence

WHAT IS TRUTH?

Just as surgeons require particular instruments in order to operate on patients without killing them, and archeologists need special tools to unearth ancient ruins without ruining them, so too, apologists must use their own unique set of tools if they want to draw others toward the truth rather than drive them further away. No matter how sincere or enthusiastic you may be, if you don't know which tools to use, your apologetics efforts will likely fail. As the famed inventor Thomas Edison once put it, "Enthusiasm is a good engine, but it needs knowledge for fuel." I've shared this maxim many times over the years with people who are just starting out in apologetics. It's a lesson I myself had to learn (and relearn) when I got my start in apologetics long ago.

There are countless untrue "truth-claims" out there competing for people's attention and allegiance. Many of them are subtle, complicated, and not easy to expose as false. But if you have the right tools and you know how to use them, you can help people shake off error and embrace the truth. Keep in mind the old saying: If the only tool you have is a hammer, you'll tend to approach every problem as if it were a nail. An apologist must rely on an array of different tools, including the Bible, the facts of history, and most important of all: logic.

It's God's grace, of course, that enables any good apologist for the Faith to be successful. And I don't mean successful in the way the world thinks of "success" (i.e., numbers, quotas, and statistics). Rather, I mean success in terms of being able to clearly, accurately, and convincingly share divine truth. The barriers of ignorance, prejudice, bad information, and lack of opportunity are almost always what prevent critics, scoffers, objectors, and dissenters from seeing and embracing the truth. Only rarely do people seem to know with certitude that something is true and yet still obstinately oppose it. Far more often people's objections are sincere, if misguided and misinformed.

That's why an apologist is really in the solutions business. He's not "selling a product." He's not trying to get someone to "buy" something. When you get right down to it, an effective apologist doesn't need to *convince* the other guy that "I'm right and you're wrong." Nobody likes to be proven wrong. So the apologist's job is to get the other guy's attention, so that when he points toward the truth, saying, "See? Isn't it wonderful? Isn't it good?" the truth's irresistible beauty and abiding gravitational pull will do the rest.

And when that happens, Jesus' promise is fulfilled in that person's heart and mind: "I am the way, the truth, and the life"; "If you continue in my word, you are truly my disciples, and you will know the truth, and the truth will make you free" (John 14:6; 8:31–32). God, especially as he has chosen to reveal himself in Jesus Christ, is the *personification* of truth. He *is* truth. And yet, that great truth is sufficiently inaccessible to us, and our limited intellects struggle to process its meaning, so we must also consider truth in the sense of the truth of things and how closely our ideas of things conform to the truth.

THE APOLOGIST'S TOOLS

You can't get people's attention if you don't know how. So now we'll consider the apologist's indispensable "tools of the trade." They'll help you remove obstacles so that people you encounter can move toward the truth. One Bible verse that's always helped remind me that it's God's grace, not human ingenuity, that makes an effective apologist is Proverbs 3:6: "In all your ways acknowledge him, and he will make straight your paths."

LOGIC AND ARGUMENTS

Let's start with the following definitions of the key tools of apologetics drawn from two respected logic textbooks,[7] followed by examples drawn from real-world apologetics discussions. The first tools we'll examine are logic and arguments.

Logic: Over the past nearly thirty years that I have been working in the field of apologetics, I have had to study logic assiduously as part of my work. Even though I have a B.Phil. in philosophy, I'm still learning from those who, like Peter Kreeft (our generation's preeminent philosopher/apologist), have dedicated their lives to teaching people how to think clearly and to use logic in defense of the Faith. So, rather than simply repeat their teaching in my own words, I'll let them explain what every apologist needs to know about the art of constructing cogent, persuasive arguments. Logic is the "science that evaluates arguments.... The aim of logic is to develop a system of methods and principles that we may use as criteria for evaluating the arguments of others and as guides in constructing arguments of our own."

Mastering the art of logic will "increase confidence that we are making sense when we criticize the arguments of others and when we advance arguments of our own."[8]

Logic enables you to construct valid arguments in defense of a truth-claim (e.g., "God exists, Jesus Christ is God"), and it helps you "troubleshoot" truth-claims (your own and those of others) by checking them for errors, also known as logical fallacies. It detects and corrects errors when they are found.

Kreeft explains how logic "powers" arguments, and how mastering the art of logic and constructing good arguments will benefit you and others:

> Logic builds the mental habit of thinking in an orderly way.... It has power: the power of proof and thus persuasion. Any power can be either rightly used or abused. This power of logic is rightly used to win the truth and defeat error; it is wrongly used to win the argument and defeat your opponent.... Logic can aid faith in at least three ways.... First, logic can clarify what is believed and define it. Second, logic can deduce the necessary *consequences* of the belief and apply it to difficult situations.... Third, even if logical arguments cannot *prove* all that faith believes, they can give firmer reasons for faith than [can] feeling, desire, mood, fashion, family or social pressure, conformity or inertia.[9]

Your apologetics efforts will be effective to the extent that they are based on good, solid arguments. By "good and solid," I mean arguments that are clear in their terms, true in their premises, and valid in their logical conclusions. If any of these three ingredients is missing, an argument is defective and will fail. You might get lucky and actually persuade an unsuspecting person with an argument that is unclear, false, or illogical, but that's being right for the wrong reasons or, something far more likely, being wrong for the wrong reasons. Kreeft explains:

> If an argument has nothing but clear terms, true premises, and valid logic, its conclusion must be true. If any one or more of these three things is lacking, we do not know whether the conclusion is true or false. It is uncertain.[10]

Let's break down this concept into its component parts. Arguments can often be reduced to syllogisms, which have three parts:

> Major premise: All squares are shapes that have four sides of equal lengths.

> Minor premise: This shape has five sides of unequal lengths.

> Conclusion: Therefore this shape is not a square.

Terms: Kreeft explains that a term "has no structural parts. It is a basic unit of meaning, like the number one in math or like an atom in the old atomic theory (when they believed atoms were unsplittable and had no parts)."[11]

A term is "clear" when its *meaning* is clear and you use it consistently according to that meaning in an argument. However, when a term is ambiguous or used in two different ways (i.e., *equivocally*), it introduces a fallacy, either because of ambiguity in meaning or because of grammatical ambiguity.

An example of ambiguity in meaning is the word "cut," which has a variety of meanings: a share in the profits, a wound made by a sharp object, being dropped from the team, a slice of meat, a cost reduction, a style of clothing fashion, a command to stop (i.e., "Cut it out!"), and so on. The phrase, "He made the cut," could refer to an athlete who is selected for a team, or a surgeon who makes an incision, or an office manager who eliminates an expense.

Or consider this recent *Wall Street Journal* headline that provides another example of ambiguity:

"GOP Lawmakers Grill IRS Chief over Lost Emails."[12]

As someone pointed out, "This type of sentence has great possibilities because of its two different interpretations: (1) Republicans harshly question the chief about the emails; and (2) Republicans cook the chief using email as the fuel."[13]

Grammatical or syntactical ambiguity occurs when the structure of a sentence renders its meaning unclear, often because of word order or because of incorrect or missing punctuation, such as: "The typical American eats more than three Greeks"; or "The police caught the man with a net." Or compare: "Please don't stop" with "Please don't! Stop!"

It's crucial to use clear, unambiguous terms when engaging in apologetics. Here's an example: the term "world" is used here, clearly and consistently:

> Jesus said, "For God so loved the *world* that he gave his only Son, that whoever believes in him should not perish but have eternal life." (John 3:16, emphasis added)

In the context of this passage *"whoever"* is universal and literal, it means everyone. Thus, you and every other human being are part of the *world* to which Jesus is referring. Therefore, because God so loves *you*, he gave his only Son so that *you* should believe in him and therefore not perish but have eternal life.

To contrast, "world" in the phrase "Athanasius against the world" (*Athanasius contra mundum*)[14] is neither universal nor literal. The great fourth-century Church Father was not literally opposed by everyone in the world in his defense of the divinity of Christ, though he was by many.

Arguments: "A group of statements, one or more of which (the premises) are claimed to provide support for, or reasons to believe, one of the others (the conclusions). All arguments may be placed in one of two basic groups: those in which the premises really do support the conclusion and those in which they do not, even though they are claimed to. The former are said to be good arguments (at least to that extent), and the latter bad arguments."[15]

Example of a good argument: When Jesus declared, "Before Abraham was, I am," the Jews "took up stones to throw at him" (John 8:59). And when Jesus said, "I and the Father are one," the "Jews took up stones again to stone him," and said, "We stone you for no good work but for blasphemy; because you, being a man, make yourself God" (John 10:30–31). Therefore, the Jews clearly understood that Jesus claimed to be God.

(The first two premises are demonstrably factual, as evidenced by the Lord's countless miracles, knowledge of the secrets of the heart, etc., described in the New Testament, and the conclusion — that Jesus is God — logically follows from those premises.)

Example of a bad argument: *Religion entails the worship of God. Most violence in the world is caused by religion. Violence, however, is incompatible with the concept of a benign "God is love" divinity. Therefore, religious violence is evidence that God does not exist.*

(The first premise is true, but the second is false, the third is ambiguous [i.e., "violence" is open to multiple meanings, such as man-caused physical violence, the violence of nature and the elements, etc.], and the conclusion does not logically follow from the premises.)

Kreeft explains these elements thus: "A term answers the question *what* it is. A proposition answers the question *whether* it is. And an argument answers the question *why* it is."

Statement/Proposition: "A sentence that is either true or false … typically a declarative sentence or a sentence component that could stand as a declarative statement."[16] The essence of apologetics is evaluating, critiquing, and demonstrating either the truth or falsity of statements/propositions made about God and His revelation to the world, as well as about everything that pertains to those "meta subjects," including the Bible, Apostolic Tradition, the Church, the sacraments, et cetera. For example,

- God exists.
- Mary did not have other children besides Jesus.
- The sacrament of Baptism regenerates the soul of the one baptized.
- The Bible does not teach the principle of *sola scriptura*.

Kreeft adds a further precision: "A proposition has two structural parts: the subject term and the predicate term. *The subject term is what you are talking about. The predicate term is what you say about the subject.* The word "subject" and "predicate" mean the same thing in logic as in grammar.[17]

Premises and Conclusions: "The statements that set forth the reasons or evidence, and … the statement that the evidence is claimed to support or imply…. [T]he conclusion is the statement that is claimed to follow from the premises."[18] In any argument, one or more of the premises must make a claim that it seeks to prove or infer explicitly in the conclusion, which is indicated with words such as "therefore" and "thus."

> Premise: Jesus Christ, who is God incarnate, promised that the gates of hell will not prevail against the Church.

> Premise: God cannot lie.

> Conclusion: Therefore, the Church Christ established will never totally apostatize.

A claim can also be logically inferred *implicitly* through premises, for example, in this way:

> The earliest Christians clearly understood what Jesus meant by saying, "This is my Body" and "This is my Blood" at the Last Supper.

> The Apostles explained to the earliest Christians all that Jesus said and did and what he meant by what he said and did.

> The Apostles knew what Jesus meant by what he said and did because they were eyewitnesses to this event and because Jesus explained everything to them (see Matthew 13:36, 16:5–12, Mark 4:34).

The next component is *validity*. For an argument to be sound, it must have clear terms, true premises (i.e. claims), and valid logic, in which case the conclusion will necessarily follow. Here are two examples of valid arguments, beginning with a classic formula:

> All men are mortal.
> Socrates is a man.
> Therefore Socrates is mortal.

All two-dimensional shapes that have three sides are triangles.

This two-dimensional shape has three sides.

Therefore this two-dimensional shape is a triangle.

Hypothesis: "A proposition, or set of propositions, set forth as an explanation for the occurrence of some specified group of phenomena, either asserted merely as a provisional conjecture to guide investigation (working hypothesis) or accepted as highly probable in the light of established facts."[19] An example of this is the hypothesis that Jesus physically rose from the dead. This proposition adequately explains why the Apostles and hundreds of others would not only proclaim that they were eyewitnesses to his Resurrection but would also be willing to suffer and die as martyrs for this conviction. The alternative hypotheses to the Resurrection, incidentally, cannot adequately account for this phenomenon.

DIFFERENT APPROACHES TO THE TRUTH

Deductive and Inductive Reasoning: The deductive approach to apologetics involves starting with general principles and working toward a specific conclusion. If the premises are true and logic is valid, the conclusion is inevitably true.

Also called "top-down" logic, deductive reasoning moves from one or more general statements (premises) to reach a logically certain conclusion. When properly formed (i.e., valid), if the premises are true, the conclusion must also be true. The earlier examples of arguments don't have necessarily true conclusions even though their premises are true because the conclusion necessarily goes beyond the premises, which is the very reason why we use those arguments. But a valid deductive argument only makes explicit what is already contained in the premises.

> All As are green.
> All Bs are As.
> Therefore, all Bs are green.

If the premise(s) is false, the logic can still be valid, though the conclusion would likewise be false. For example, it could be that, in fact, some As are red, in which case the first premise ("all As are green") would be false.

> All Catholics are hypocrites.
> William is Catholic.
> Therefore William is a hypocrite.

The Inductive Approach: The fictional detective Sherlock Holmes is known to countless readers as a genius for figuring out obscure and complex crimes on the basis of drawing conclusions from minute and easily overlooked details. He exemplifies the inductive reasoning approach. The popular television show *Monk* is another example of inductive logic at work.

Examples of inductive reasoning in apologetics would include:

> 1. Tabulating all the times Simon Peter is mentioned by name in the New Testament (195 times), and then comparing that statistic to the number of times the next most often mentioned Apostle is named (John, 29 times), suggests that Simon Peter was the most prominent figure among the Twelve Apostles.

2. Noting that things continually come into and go out of existence and are therefore contingent (i.e., unnecessary) and do not have to exist because at one point they did not exist. But yet they do exist. This suggests that there must be a being, which we call God, who must necessarily exist in order to explain the existence of this vast number of contingent, unnecessary beings.

3. Examining all the details of the life of Jesus Christ as they are presented in the pages of the New Testament — his miracles, teachings, reading the secrets of the heart, claims to be God, claims to forgive sins, and rising from the dead — so as to draw the conclusion that he is in fact truly God and not merely a man.

The Apophatic Approach: From the Greek ἀπόφασις (*apóphatis*), meaning "denial."[20] The apophatic approach uses *negation* to arrive at a clearer understanding of the truth. By asserting things that are not true, you can clear away erroneous and misleading claims that deny or obscure the truth. Examples of true statements that are expressed negatively in order to eliminate erroneous alternatives:

- God is *not* evil; He is *not* limited; He is *not* subject to change.
- God is *not* the author of evil.
- Human beings do *not* have the natural ability to save themselves from damnation.
- The Holy Spirit is *not* merely an impersonal "force."

- Receiving Holy Communion is *not* "cannibalism."
- The Holy Bible *nowhere* claims to be the sole, sufficient rule of Faith for Christians.

The Kataphatic Approach: From the Greek καταφατικό (*kataphatikó*), meaning "affirmative." The opposite of apophatic, the kataphatic approach *affirms* certain truths that make other truths clearer. Examples of such affirmations in an apologetic setting:

- God *is* all good (omnibenevolent), all knowing (omniscient), all powerful (omnipotent).
- Everything God creates *is* good.[21]
- The Bible declares that Tradition *is* necessary and important.
- Jesus *is* Lord.
- Unaided by Divine revelation, the human intellect *is* capable of arriving at the fact that God exists.

DEMONSTRATIVE AND PROBABLE EVIDENCE

Every apologetics encounter involves an appeal to evidence of some sort. Evidence (i.e., facts, data, information, artifacts, documentation, testimony, etc.) is the "raw material" of apologetics. The method of argumentation is the blueprint or schematic that conforms that raw material into an instrument that conveys truth. In apologetics, this instrument also functions as a monument or sign that points toward those true conclusions that are warranted or even necessitated by the evidence.

For example: Your coworker insists that Jesus never existed and that the "Jesus myth" is simply the result of centuries of stories, folklore, and fables that began with the chicanery of the earliest Christians who sought (successfully) to dupe people into believing in a "Jesus" who never really existed so that they could garner power, wealth, and influence.

You respond to this claim with an appeal to evidence in the form of historical documents written by Jewish and pagan authors who, being contemporaries or near contemporaries of the Apostles, corroborate the fact that Jesus actually existed in a particular place and time. You then show how the corroborating evidence provided by those non-Christian sources matches the chronology and geography of the descriptions of Jesus' life and times in the Gospels. Your truth-claim (i.e., Jesus really *did* exist and was not a myth) is based on historical evidence presented with an argument from authority (i.e., those authoritative Jewish and pagan writers [whose own existence is unquestioned] verify that Jesus actually existed) that entails the following deduction:

> If someone as spectacular and intriguing as Jesus really existed, some contemporary witnesses would have written about him.
>
> Some contemporary witnesses *did* write about him.
>
> Therefore, it is reasonable to conclude that Jesus really existed.

The alternative conclusion would be that even though various contemporary authors (who did not know each other) did write about Jesus as a real historical person, he did not really exist and they wrote about him for ... what? For no reason? Multiple contemporaries separated by language, cultures, and great distances, for some reason all independently decided to write historical fiction about a previously unknown character? This conclusion is illogical in that it does not follow from the evidence.

This is an example of what's known as "evidential apologetics," which, historically, has been the most common and most effective method of defending Christianity. A minor and far more recent counterpart to the classical evidential apologetics is known in Protestant (especially Calvinist/Reformed) circles as "presuppositional apologetics,"[22] which seeks to prove Christian truths by way of first presupposing the "self-attesting" divinity of Jesus Christ and the "self-attesting" nature of the Bible as inspired, inerrant revelation. While it is certainly true that Jesus *is* true God and true man and the Holy Bible *is* divinely inspired and inerrant, the presuppositional apologetics technique[23] is generally less effective than the evidentialist approach. But it is also inadequate as a means of engaging modern culture with its relentless demand for "evidence" before it will believe in something.[24]

Avery Dulles, S.J., describes presuppositional apologetics, as "practiced by Protestants," as a position that "normally rests on the premise that human reason has been so damaged by sin that evidential apologetics is useless. Presuppositionalists therefore begin by assuming that the teaching of the Bible is true. Setting out from this axiom, the apologist argues that biblical revelation yields a coherent explanation of our experience in the world and that other worldviews are, in comparison, incoherent. Some add that it is impossible to live or think without logically presupposing the reality of God, the source and measure of all truth."[25] One of my own books, *The Godless Delusion* (coauthored with Kenneth Hensley), is a kind of hybrid between presuppositional and evidentialist apologetics, incorporating the useful elements of the former (e.g., that the existence of God sufficiently explains the reality of incorporeal realities such as truth, love, and knowledge and that atheism cannot adequately explain them) and welding them to the evidentialist chassis of making the case for God by an appeal to the overwhelming evidence that he exists.

The evidentialist approach to apologetics seeks to make use of principles of evidence that are commonly agreed upon by both Christians and non-Christians, even atheists, e.g., historical evidence, eyewitness testimony, et cetera. As we have seen, the two primary categories of arguments are deductive and inductive.

Deductive arguments are structured as either a *modus ponens* (Latin: a way of putting) or a *modus tolens* (a way of taking). An example of the former is:

> If Jesus performed miracles such as raising people from the dead, then it seems likely that he was more than a mere human being — possibly God.

> Jesus *did* raise people from the dead.

> Therefore it seems likely that he was more than a more human being — possibly God.

An example of the latter approach (*modus tolens*) is:

> If the Apostles were lying about Jesus rising from the dead (knowing that he did not rise), it seems likely that they lied for some kind of personal gain, such as wealth, concubines, worldly prestige, et cetera.

> The Apostles did not gain wealth, concubines, or worldly prestige but were, instead, scorned,

hunted, and eventually martyred because of their message about Jesus.

Therefore, the Apostles were not lying about Jesus' Resurrection.

When you make an apologetics argument based on documentary evidence, such as an appeal to early pagan, Jewish, or Christian authors to corroborate your claim that Jesus was a real historical person, the more examples you offer the better they help to corroborate and support your hypothesis. Another example would be that the early Church believed in the Real Presence of Christ in the Eucharist. To make this case, you should adduce quotations to that effect from significant and authoritative early witnesses such as St. Ignatius of Antioch, St. Justin Martyr, St. Irenaeus of Lyons, St. Cyril of Jerusalem, et cetera. Providing multiple examples to support your position is far more compelling than a single example, which may or may not be adequate support.

Be aware of and be prepared for counterexamples. For example, when you explain the biblical doctrine of the interlocking, interdependent nature of *Scripture and Tradition in the Church*[26] by quoting passages that demonstrate the importance and necessity of Apostolic Tradition (e.g., 1 Corinthians 11:2, 2 Thessalonians 2:15, etc.), be prepared for counterexamples that may be raised against Tradition, such as Matthew 15:1-9, Mark 7:1-14, and Colossians 2:20-23. If you have carefully prepared a response to those counterargument verses, you will not be flustered or deterred when they are raised.

Remember also arguments from correlation — that is, causes and effects. A good example would be if someone raises the objection against Catholic Marian doctrines such as the Immaculate Conception or Mary's role as the

Mother of God (Greek: Θεοτοκος; Latin: *Mater Dei*). You should explain the correlation between the relative absence of writings about these Marian doctrines during the first two centuries of the Church and the fact that the Church in the Roman Empire experienced successive waves of severe persecution that prevented its theologians from writing on this topic because the Church was fighting for its very survival and did not have the opportunity to develop those theological truths.

Remember also that correlated issues are not necessarily related: for example, the arguments raised about alleged Catholic/pagan similarities, and so forth. It does not necessarily follow that because there is a similarity there is a correlation, much less a direct cause-effect relationship.

The art of apologetics is multifaceted, and its applications can be quite diverse. But don't let that throw you, especially if you're just starting out in your study of how to explain and defend the Faith. Just as an experienced golfer has learned from experience and practice which of the fourteen different clubs in his golf bag to use at any given point on the course, so too you'll learn which apologetics tools will work best for any given apologetics situation in which you find yourself. And happily, as any veteran apologist will tell you, it's not that difficult to tell them apart and know when (and when not) to use them.

Because there's no "one size fits all" approach to apologetics, you'll need to understand which apologetics tools to rely on in a given apologetics situation.

CHAPTER 4

From Atheists to Dissenters

An Overview of Issues

Allow me to give you brief overviews of certain aspects of apologetics with different types of people. These synopses are not intended to elaborate all the essential issues, nor show how to resolve them, but rather to give the aspiring apologist a general sense of the issues he or she will need to be familiar with in order to engage in apologetics with people in those groups. The trajectory follows the three levels of apologetics starting with the most fundamental: natural apologetics (God), Christian apologetics (Jesus), Catholic apologetics (the Church).

APOLOGETICS WITH ATHEISTS

Obviously, because atheists deny the existence of God and anything supernatural (e.g., heaven and hell, human souls, angels and demons), only the most basic level of apologetics — *natural* — is possible or appropriate when engaging them. This means that your efforts to find common ground must begin with God's existence. It would be pointless to present to an atheist an apologetics defense of, say, the Holy Eucharist. This is not to say that *at some point* you couldn't explain the Eucharist, the divinity of Christ, or the authenticity of the Bible, but you'll first need to lay a solid foundation for believing in God's existence. Just like building a house, you start with the foundation and work your way up.

APOLOGETICS WITH THE CULTURE

Defending the Faith sometimes requires that you engage the culture itself. It propagates those errors in the media that infect great numbers of people with *attitudes* and *assumptions* that can obscure their view of reality.

Moral relativism is a perfect example of what I mean. Doing apologetics in an environment where many people have been conditioned for many years to think that truth is relative ("That may be true for you, but it's not true for me") can be exceedingly challenging. The moral relativist mind-set sees issues like abortion, gay marriage, homosexual activity, adultery, fornication, pornography, and contraception as merely personal preference options, not activities that can be called "right" or "wrong." Or more exactly, while one can say such activities are right, it's absolutely unacceptable to say they are morally wrong. It's a one-way street.

Your best tools in this area of apologetics will be logic and the ability to spot fallacies, because moral relativism is itself a fallacy and it both feeds on fallacious, uncritical thinking and continually spawns it in modern culture.

Before you can engage in apologetics on moral issues, you must first help someone see that "morals" as such exist at all. They are above us, transcendent, and not dependent upon our personal whims and preferences. Happily, it's not terribly difficult to use basic logic to point out the internal incoherence of moral relativism by simply relativizing something the other guy is passionate about.

For example, a woman once angrily scolded me for being "antiabortion" and "selfish" because my wife and I have eleven children. A friend and I were standing in the checkout line at a store, and, while chatting, it happened to come up that we have a lot of kids. The lady ahead of me, hearing this, whirled around with an angry look on her face and informed me emphatically that I was selfish because our family was taking up resources, crowding the planet, and so on. "You're antiabortion, I'll bet!" she said with a sneer. And I responded, "Yes, I am. Abortion is immoral." This, as you might guess, made her madder. She said, "Get over it! Abortion is legal!"

"What does it being legal have to do with it?" I countered. "Just because it's legal doesn't mean it's not immoral."

"It wouldn't *be* legal if it were immoral!" she snapped back.

That's when I realized what I needed to do.

I decided to use a logic move known as the *reductio ad absurdum* in which you take the person's claim at face value and, by asking questions, reduce it to its absurd and intolerable logical conclusion.

So, I asked her, "Well, what about slavery? That used to be legal in the United States. It used to be perfectly legal for white people to own black people; to buy and sell them, split up their families — separate husbands from their wives, parents from their children — and to work them literally to death. Are you saying that slavery was not immoral simply because it was *legal*?"

She glared at me but said nothing, so I continued.

"And what about the Third Reich's laws mandating the extermination of millions of Jews and others during World War II? Did that make those actions moral just because they happened to be legal?"

By now, a vein in this woman's forehead was throbbing. But still she said nothing. So I fired off one more example for good measure. I asked her how she felt about the fact that until the passage of the nineteenth Amendment it was perfectly legal for men to prevent women from voting. "Did the fact that this was legal make it right?"

At that, she stormed off. All I could do was pray for her and hope that my line of argumentation got through her defensive shields about a "woman's right to abortion." I had to come at this issue from a vantage point she was completely unprepared to defend against. I hope that conversation made enough of a dent in her worldview for the grace of God to enter her heart and start transforming her. That's just one example of how when you engage the culture in defense of truth, Bible verses and the facts of Christian history are probably not your best tools. More often than not, what you'll need to use are the tools of logic and analogies. Those really do work in that kind of situation.

APOLOGETICS WITH NON-CHRISTIANS (JEWS, MUSLIMS, HINDUS, BUDDHISTS, ETC.)

Non-Christians who believe in God already have common ground with you. Build on this by seeking areas of agreement on issues such as morality, truth, religious obligation, and so on. Keep in mind that you will find a very different set of issues from one religion to another. Islam's moral code is quite different in certain respects from that of Buddhism — the concept of radical jihad being an example. Non-Christian world religions can be monotheistic (e.g., Judaism, Islam, Sikhism), polytheistic (e.g., Hinduism, Shinto, Jainism), and, in the case of Buddhism, not focused on knowing, worshipping, or even believing in a personal God. Apologetics in this field focuses on the person and uniqueness of Jesus Christ, his existence, miracles, teachings, Resurrection, and divinity.

APOLOGETICS WITH MORMONS, JEHOVAH'S WITNESSES

These two groups are, in most ways, extremely different but in some ways extremely similar. Both deny central Christian doctrines — Mormons deny monotheism and the Trinity, Jehovah's Witnesses affirm monotheism but deny the Trinity and the divinity of Jesus Christ and the Holy Spirit. As a result, even though both religions have completely appropriated Christian terminology, their doctrines are not Christian. Rather than classify them in the non-Christian world religions category, I've found it's more helpful to understand them as "quasi-Christian." In other words, their beliefs at their core are not Christian and yet they both profess to believe in Jesus Christ, both claim the New Testament as an authority, and both formulate their doctrines using Christian terminology.

Unfortunately, there are currently no substantive books written by adequately prepared Catholics responding to Jehovah's Witnesses. However, Catholic Answers has a wealth of materials in the form of articles and tracts that delve deeply into the peculiar arguments you will likely encounter when doing apologetics with them. You can get them by visiting catholic.com and putting "Jehovah's Witnesses" in the search bar.

As for doing apologetics with Mormons, I recommend Isaiah Bennett's *Inside Mormonism*. This book may be out of print, but you can still find used copies on the Internet. I have written a number of basic apologetics articles on Mormonism that are available in the "articles" section of patrickmadrid.com, and there you can also download the audio of two public debates I did with Mormon leaders. Many more articles on Mormonism are available for free at catholic.com.

Also check out Lighthouse Catholic Media's 3-CD set *Inside Mormonism* and the single CD *From Mormon Missionary to the Catholic Faith*, by former Mormon Thomas Smith. These are available at LighthouseCatholicMedia.org. The late Fr. William Mitchell, a Catholic priest, wrote a basic, introductory apologetics book on Mormonism called *A Christian Looks at Mormonism*, which is available electronically at transporter.com, the website of Steve Clifford, a former Mormon who converted to the Catholic Church.

APOLOGETICS WITH PROTESTANTS

Since there are many different doctrinal variations on the Protestant theme, this is a broad category. Protestantism as such is not a monolithic belief system in which everyone professes the same set of teachings, so I can only give you general principles here. Later in this book, I'll delve deeper into the specific kinds of issues to raise when doing apologetics with Christians who love Jesus and read the Bible but don't agree with the Catholic Church.

First, this is perhaps the easiest area for apologetics because Catholics and Protestants already have a great deal of common ground to start with and build upon. Belief in a personal, loving God? Check. Belief in the Trinity and divinity of Christ? Check. Salvation in Jesus alone by grace alone? Check.[27] Belief in the authority of the Bible? Check. Heaven and hell, angels and devils, good and evil? Check, check, check. There's a great deal of commonality to work with.

So, how do you work it? With Protestants, you'll need clear thinking and good logical arguments, but most of all you'll need to make your case from the Bible and from the facts of Christian history. I'll show you in more detail how to do this a little later.

APOLOGETICS WITH EASTERN ORTHODOX

These situations usually require a knowledge of the long and tangled history of the Catholic Church in the Western Roman Empire and how it developed differently in certain respects (linguistically, liturgically, and theologically) in the East, the lands which today are where the Eastern Orthodox Churches are located.[28] The age-old disputes between the Eastern Churches and the Catholic Church in the West led to a gradual and then complete estrangement. Disagreements over the *filioque* clause in the Latin version of the Nicene Creed looms large as a theological dispute, as does the role and authority of the papacy and the relationship of the Bishop of Rome to other patriarchs and bishops. There are also lesser though still serious difficulties over the doctrines of purgatory and the Immaculate Conception of the Blessed Virgin Mary, as well as disagreements on the subject of divorce and remarriage. The Greek Orthodox Church, for example, permits divorce and remarriage. The Catholic Church does not.[29]

APOLOGETICS WITH CATHOLICS

This subsection of apologetics can be especially tricky because debating a truth of the Faith with a fellow Catholic seems to question their Catholicity. And that's not at all the case. You should never imply that the other person isn't *really* Catholic just because he or she doesn't fully understand a given truth. Before we get into some real-world examples of what I'm talking about, let me first add an important word of caution: Don't allow yourself to slip into the mode of thinking that you are the "orthodoxy police" or imagine that it's your duty to root out theological error wherever you can find it. This attitude will subtly engender a destructive "search and destroy" mentality, rather than a virtuous "search and rescue" approach. You will also very likely find it difficult to get a hearing once people feel like you're just waiting for an opportunity to pounce so you can judge and correct them. I mention this issue because it's a surprisingly common occupational hazard among those who learn apologetics at a deeper level. Without even realizing it's happening, even some longtime apologists still manage to come across as if they are a one-man walking magisterium. Don't be that guy.

As we've seen, apologetics should always be about serving others and never about one's personal need to always have the right answer or the last word.

THOSE WHO FORGET WHAT THEY ONCE KNEW

One example of apologetics that comes immediately to mind happened to me a long time ago during an apologetics seminar I conducted at a large suburban parish. During the Q&A session, a man in his late sixties asked me the following question:

"I serve as an extraordinary minister of Holy Communion at daily Mass and don't know what to do about a few people in the congregation who receive *only* the host at Communion. They always bypass the chalice and don't receive the Precious Blood. They don't seem to realize they aren't receiving the '*whole Jesus*'!" His frustration at this "problem" was palpable, and I was dismayed to see several other older people in the audience nodding in agreement with his concern.

I did the best I could to tactfully and *gently* disabuse this gentleman of his apprehension. I explained to him that the Catholic Church does *not* teach that one receives the "whole Jesus" in Communion only if he or she consumes both the sacred host and a sip of the Precious Blood. I pointed out that the Church teaches exactly the opposite. Even the smallest portion of the host or the slightest sip of the Precious Blood contains "all" of Jesus sacramentally and substantially present under the appearances of bread and wine. No doubt, this devout man (a daily communicant, no less!) had simply forgotten this piece of Catholic teaching somewhere along the way. The best thing for an apologist to do in that situation would be to offer a gentle recalibration of the questioner's understanding of the doctrine so that the part he had forgotten would come back into view. I have a theory that's taken shape in my mind over the years I've spent speaking to Catholics all across the country. I have observed that *most* church-going adult Catholics have about an eighth-grade level of understanding of Catholic doctrines.[30] This is not meant to be at all condescending. Think about it: The average Catholic stops any type of formal, systematic training in Church teaching at about the time he or she gets confirmed. People get busy with life and simply don't make the time for further study. It's no wonder, then, that many Catholics have become a little hazy about aspects of Church teaching after three, four, or five decades with nary a CCD class since being confirmed.

THOSE WHO DISSENT

One of Catholic media's pet buzzwords nowadays is "culture-wars." Like other hackneyed catchphrases ("worship space," "faith journey") it's ambiguous and tendentious. And it often misses the mark when employed as a descriptor of the blight of overt, intentional doctrinal dissent among some Catholics and the efforts of other Catholics to help them "get their minds right" on said doctrines.

It refers to the ongoing friction between Catholics who freely assent to the totality of Catholic teaching and those who dissent from one or more Church teachings (especially on holy orders being reserved to men and on life issues, such as abortion, contraception, and homosexual activity) and yet remain in the Catholic Church and seek to "change it" from the inside. These doctrinal disagreements are surely problematic, and it requires a somewhat different kind of apologetics approach to try to overcome them.

Whereas it's efficacious to use the Bible in discussions with Protestants, many Catholic dissenters from Catholic teaching will simply dismiss a scriptural argument as being irrelevant because it was written in a "patriarchal milieu." Or they might argue that your "medieval" interpretation just isn't up to date with modern "insights" into the text. And they may respond with a radically different (and radically defective) counterinterpretation of a passage as a way to blunt the effect of your biblical argument.

For example, some argue that the fire-and-brimstone punishment God inflicted upon Sodom and Gomorrah had nothing to do with homosexual immorality but was meted out because of "failure to show hospitality to strangers." The easiest and most effective way I have found to counter this erroneous interpretation is to ask a few questions:

> How do you account for the fact that Lot and his family *did* show hospitality to the angelic strangers? He took them into his home, fed them, gave them a place to sleep for the night, and protected them from the "the men of the city, the men of Sodom, both young and old, all the people to the last man, [who] surrounded the house; and they called to Lot, 'Where are

the men who came to you tonight? Bring them out to us, that we may know them[31]" (Genesis 19:5).

Where does the Law of Moses prescribe *death* as a penalty for those who fail to offer hospitality to strangers? (Answer: It doesn't. See Leviticus 20 for the list of offenses that were punishable by death under the Mosaic Law.)

Where do we see any place in the Bible where God killed an individual man or woman or destroyed a whole city expressly because they didn't roll out the welcome wagon? (Answer: Nowhere. If the person you're debating cites Genesis 19, point out that it's exactly that passage that doesn't show this view.)

How does one account for the fact that the two angels in this passage explicitly state exactly why the cities will be destroyed and the reason they give is *not* the lack of hospitality? "We are about to destroy this place, *because the outcry against its people has become great before the* LORD, and the LORD has sent us to destroy it" (Genesis 9:13). The two angels had only just arrived in the city. There was no time for an outcry against the inhabitants of the city to become so great before God that he inflicted punishment against it if it was only for lack of hospitality toward the angels.

To conclude this chapter, let's focus on the *limitations* of apologetics. There are many. The foremost among them are your own human limitations of knowledge and ability. This is nothing to be bothered about because God delights in making use of our limitations and weaknesses. But just be aware that no matter how proficient you may become at apologetics, there is always room for improvement. St. Thomas Aquinas, one of the most effective apologists, recognized how much better he could have done in defending the truth. Just before his death in 1274, God granted him a vision in which He told the friar, "You have written well of me, Thomas. What reward would you have for your labor?" St. Thomas's answer was simply, "Nothing but you, Lord." Shortly after that, Thomas confided to a brother friar that all he had written "seems like straw to me" (*mihi videtur ut palea*).

Other limitations of apologetics include the intellectual and emotional weaknesses of opponents and the intricacy and complexity of some doctrines, such as the Trinity and the divinity of Christ. The fact that apologetics is always, by nature, going to be limited should never discourage you. Rather, it should *encourage* you to learn more and become more proficient so that you can be that much more efficacious in helping people come closer to God and all truth. For, as Jesus promised, "With men it is impossible, but not with God; for all things are possible with God" (Mark 10:27).

CHAPTER 5

The Art of Practical Apologetics

Essential Strategies and Effective Tactics

As a teenager, I liked the popular TV show *Kung Fu*, mainly for its fight scenes, which always played out in slow motion. What I liked best was how the main character, Kwai Chang Kaine, defeated his opponents, not by attacking them, but by using their own forward momentum against them. He often stepped aside as they lunged at him, redirecting them straight into a brick wall. Kaine's Kung Fu skills seemed to be more about self-defense than aggression. In a similar way, doing apologetics often works like that. You learn how to handle arguments against your position more gracefully and effectively. We'll start by considering some of the barriers to apologetics.

EMOTION

No human being is free of emotions. These often mysterious movements of the soul that arouse in us feelings of joy, affection, contentment, boredom, fear, anxiety, and sadness are like the weather. At times they linger; at times they sweep over us suddenly and pass by quickly. As the late Fr. Jordon Aumann, O.P., explained, "Emotions are psychosomatic reactions of the individual and hence closely related to temperament ... sanguine, melancholic, choleric, and phlegmatic."[32]

Our emotions (i.e., passions) can affect how well or poorly we explain the truth as much as they can affect how a person responds to the truth. For instance, if you're angry when doing apologetics — you know, really provoked by the other person's mean-spirited anti-Catholicism — it will be difficult for you to express yourself calmly. This is just as true if the other guy is feeling that way about you. Sometimes, when negative emotions are running high, it's best to just defer the conversation to a later time when you're both more able to speak and listen constructively.

For example, when I was just getting into apologetics, I was driving somewhere with a Protestant coworker named Keith. An ardent Southern Baptist, Keith was also very interested in apologetics, though from the Protestant (and decidedly anti-Catholic) side of the fence. Because the company we worked for frequently sent us on assignments together, we had plenty of time to discuss religion while in transit, and our discussions were invariably energetic. Once our conversation became particularly heated as we argued over biblical authority.

Keith was going on about how the Catholic Church added "nonbiblical traditions of men," something he'd hit me with repeatedly before. Naturally, I was irritated by his continued harangue on this theme, but this time was different because I had been studying carefully how to counter this argument. I started challenging his claim with Bible verses, such as 1 Corinthians 11:2 and 2 Thessalonians 2:15, which expressly show that the Protestant principle of *sola scriptura* (i.e., the Bible alone) is actually unbiblical, that Apostolic Tradition is also part of the Deposit of Faith "once for all handed on to the saints" (Jude 3), and that Keith's claim was based on a demonstrably false assumption about biblical authority. At this point, his forward momentum in the argument slowed to a stop and turned in my favor.

My mistake, though, was to press my advantage too aggressively. By now, Keith sat in silence as I barraged *him* with passages of Scripture that undercut his "Bible alone" argument. Although he said nothing, his face flushed and he shook his head emphatically as I spoke. The more he did that, the louder and more forceful and — I hate to admit it — the more *condescending* I became until he couldn't take it anymore.

"Shut *up!*" he shouted at me angrily, the vein in his neck popping and his hands tightly gripping the steering wheel in white-knuckle frustration. "Just shut up, okay? You're wrong! And just because you quote a lot of Bible verses doesn't make you right!"

Wow, I thought to myself in shock and surprise. I had no idea he'd react so fiercely, especially since we had argued about the Bible many times before, though never with anywhere near this level of acrimony.

Now it was my turn to say nothing. We rode in an uncomfortable silence for the next couple of minutes, and I tried to figure out how to proceed without inflaming things any worse.

"Keith, I didn't mean to insult you or make you mad, but…."

"Well, you *are* making me mad because of your stupid arguments and misquoting of the Bible!" he shot back. "You're quoting those passages out of context and trying to undermine the authority of the Word of God so you can defend your Catholic 'traditions of men.' That's wrong, and yes, that makes me mad when Catholics do that."

I wish I could report that I found an effective way to soothe the situation and get Keith to listen to my point of view, but that didn't happen. I tried to remind him that, as far as I was concerned, all he had been doing was quoting the Bible out of context and trying to cow me into submission, if not agreement. But that just made it worse. He didn't say anything now, and we rode along in silence. Not only was that the end of that particular conversation, it was the end of our acquaintance. We avoided each other after that.

What I learned from this misadventure was the potentially destructive power of negative emotions in apologetics, both his and my own. Because we were both angry, and had been for some time, my attempts at apologetics that day were counterproductive. My mistake was, upon realizing that Keith was at a loss to defend against my arguments, to lunge in for the "kill" in a way that screamed "search and destroy!" rather than calmly saying, "Hey, please try to consider a different way of looking at things." The intrusion of emotions ruined the conversation and any subsequent opportunity I might have had to win him over to the Catholic Church. Footnote: I looked Keith up on Facebook recently and saw that, thirty-plus years later, he's still an ardent Southern Baptist.

The memory of my apologetics failure that day has never left me. I share it with you here in hopes you'll avoid the same mistakes I made by keeping a close reign on your own emotions when you do apologetics.

A final thought about emotion is that it can also be your friend when doing apologetics, especially when you can seek to instill a sense of friendship and respect by remaining calm, cheerful, and polite. I've found that even the most antagonistic critics can be pacified with a good dose of genuine courtesy and lots of patience. As the Bible says, "A soft answer turns away wrath" (Proverbs 15:1).

EXPERIENCE

Some people have had negative experiences with the Catholic Church and have become very closed to it as a result. This, like negative emotions, will usually make your efforts to explain and defend the faith more difficult, but not impossible. Often, people who reject the Faith can trace their distrust and misgivings all the way back to an event in their childhood. Whether it's caused by something as horrible as abuse, or something less devastating, such as "a priest yelled at me in confession," or perhaps a Catholic boss who gave scandal through hypocrisy or a run-in with someone at the parish, there are many ways that people's negative experiences can create immense barriers of suspicion. But even these can be dismantled, little by little, with the right approach, which usually involves three ingredients:

1. Validating the other person's feelings of being wronged by Catholics[33]

2. A sincere apology on your part for things other Catholics have done to cause hurt and alienation from the Church[34]

3. A humble and sincere invitation to reconsider the Church in light of the evidence, rather than through the lens of the past hurt

IMAGINATION

Human beings are unique among all creatures in the universe because we are the only ones composed of matter and spirit (body and soul). For this reason, we acquire understanding of things through the medium of our five senses. The intellect abstracts information from the senses and forms "phantasms" (mental pictures) of things from which it then derives universal concepts. For example, the first time you see a horse you understand it as *that thing* called a "horse." But once you've seen another horse, and another, you understand the universal category of "horseness" that transcends each individual horse. The imagination is very powerful indeed in making these mental images that enable us to contemplate and better understand the world around us. Just so, the imagination can be both a help and an impediment to apprehending the truth.

On the plus side, the imagination helps us draw conclusions and understand deeper meanings by giving us a mental image of the thing. For example, we can more readily understand the regenerating and cleansing effects of the sacrament of Baptism because we've seen how water washes things, removing dirt and making them clean. Our sensory experience of physical hunger and thirst enables us to easily understand in a spiritual sense what Jesus meant by "Blessed are those who hunger and thirst for righteousness, for they shall be satisfied" (Matthew 5:6).

The down side of the imagination, however, kicks in when someone has difficulty forming a mental image of something that is true, such as the Blessed Trinity, but for which the senses have nothing to compare with. There is no *thing* you've ever seen or touched that is comprised of one nature shared by three persons. You have no experience of this. Which means, the best you can do as a human being is struggle to think of the Trinity in the purely abstract, which is exceedingly difficult; or you can make use of mental analogies as a way to get a metaphorical understanding of it. The most common example of this is when we think of the

Triune God as an assemblage of three figures: a venerable old man with a white beard (Father), Jesus Christ (Son), and a white dove (the Holy Spirit). It's a mental image of something we have never seen. And, it's the best most of us can manage.

"But getting rid of the pictures," Catholic apologist Frank Sheed wrote, "is of value only if, in their place, we develop a truer idea of God; otherwise, we have merely a blank where the picture used to hang."[35]

So, when doing apologetics, it's important to recognize when it's appropriate to engage the imagination. Word pictures, analogies, metaphors, and similes are all legitimate and valuable tools of apologetics, provided they are employed carefully and with due regard for their inherent limitations.

An analogy is way of comparing two different things that are similar in some way, and the comparison between the two yields deeper insights. It is defined as "a form of reasoning in which one thing is inferred to be similar to another thing in a certain respect, on the basis of the known similarity between the things in other respects."[36]

A metaphor is "a figure of speech in which a term or phrase is applied to something to which it is not literally applicable in order to suggest a resemblance, as in 'A mighty fortress is our God.'"[37]

The Bible itself begins with an analogy: "So God created man in his own image, in the image of God he created him; male and female he created them" (Genesis 1:27). The creature, man, is like his creator, not by nature, but by similarity. The analogy here is not one of "physical" resemblance, for God does not have a body of flesh and blood as human beings do. Rather we are like God (i.e., analogous to Him) and have been made in His image because we have an intellect and a will, just as He does. Like Him, we have the capacity to know what is true and do what is good.

Metaphors abound in Scripture, including Jesus' well-known teachings, "I am the vine, you are the branches," and "You are the salt of the earth;... You are the light of the world. A city set on a hill cannot be hidden. Nor do men light a lamp and put it under a bushel [basket], but on a stand, and it gives light to all in the house. Let your light so shine before men, that they may see your good works and give glory to your Father who is in heaven" (Matthew 5:13–16).

Because our limited human intellects must work very hard to delve deeper into realties with which we have no direct experience, it's important for the apologist to make proper use of analogies and metaphors to help people bridge the gap. Jesus did this constantly in his teaching and preaching, as did St. Paul in his.[38]

ANALOGIES FOR THE TRINITY

Another classic example is St. Patrick's legendary (in both senses of the word) use of the analogy of a three-leaf shamrock in his efforts to explain the Blessed Trinity, that is, how God can be three persons sharing one nature. Everyone Patrick preached to had seen a shamrock and, thereby, gained a somewhat better insight into the Trinity by use of this analogy, even though its use is limited at best. Three leaves are three parts of a single thing, and that is not true of God.[39] Even so, our limited human intellects, and our even more limited imagination *can* gain a toehold on the sheer face of reality through the use of analogies like this. They can't adequately explain, much less literally *show us*, the eternal realities we seek to understand, but they point us in the right direction and offer us a faint outline to help us along.

The truth is, we cannot avoid using analogies, such as the analogy of being, when trying to explain and defend the Trinity because human language is based on analogous terms, terms which are grounded in temporality and the natural realities we live within (i.e., time and space).[40] We necessarily must employ such language in our efforts to speak about God Himself, who is utterly transcendent. In human language, we must find a philosophical way to speak of such things.

St. Augustine was a master of analogies when teaching deep theological concepts, such as the Trinity. His classic *De Trinitate* (*On the Trinity*) relies heavily on analogies to help his readers comprehend how God can be radically one in nature and yet three divine Persons. A great deal of Augustine's effort was expended in defense of doctrines that are much easier to accept when they are explained by things we can see and touch. His defense of the Faith against the Manichean Heresy is replete with such examples.

The Manicheans held that the universe is dualistic, good and bad, spiritual and material, light and dark. It was easier for many in Augustine's day to *imagine* that earthly, physical things are part of the realm of evil and darkness because everyone understood physical things like toothaches, headaches, hunger, stubbed toes, and childbirth. It is much harder to imagine how it is that God makes full use of both matter and spirit to accomplish his loving purposes. For that matter, it's much more difficult to imagine how God could become one of us in the Incarnation. That's why much of St. Augustine's apologetics toward the Manicheans dealt with explaining how "the Word became flesh and dwelt among us" (John 1:14).

Over the years that I've been doing apologetics, I've found that Jehovah's Witnesses and Mormons are two groups in particular whose members seem especially resistant to the doctrine of the Trinity. They have a hard time trying to imagine one God in three divine Persons. More than one Jehovah's Witness has personally admitted this to me in doorstep discussions. It's just easier to imagine one God in one Person. And once that concept is firmly accepted as the only acceptable one, it's difficult to dislodge it with the truth.

The Jehovah's Witnesses made a big splash in the 1990s with a comic-book-sized publication called *Should You Believe in the Trinity?*[41] This excerpt from the booklet exemplifies what I mean by the limits of imagination being an obstacle to apologetics:

> Many sincere believers have found [the Trinity doctrine] to be confusing, contrary to normal reason, *unlike anything in their experience.* How, they ask, could the Father be God, Jesus be God, and the holy spirit [sic] be God, yet there be not three Gods but only one God? This confusion is widespread.... Countless pages have been written attempting to explain it. Yet, after struggling through the labyrinth of confusing theological terms and explanations, investigators still come away unsatisfied.[42]

Mormons, too, reject the Trinity, though for radically different reasons than do Jehovah's Witnesses. Whereas the latter hold to a radical monotheism, denying the Trinity and the divinity of Christ and the Holy Spirit, the former proclaim a polytheistic belief in a "plurality of Gods" who are utterly distinct as separate beings. One Mormon critic of the Trinity scoffed, "The Trinity: Try to understand it and you'll lose your mind; try to deny it and you'll lose your soul."

Like Jehovah's Witnesses and Mormons, other groups such as the Iglesia ni Cristo and Muslims reject the Trinity in large part because they cannot imagine it. So, in your apologetics endeavors, remember the importance and the liability of the imagination. Use analogies judiciously so you can help someone "see" a bit more clearly what you're trying to explain. But don't forget that sometimes, as with the Trinity, doing so can be very difficult. In such cases, it's helpful to explain that we believe in many abstract realities, such as the human soul, honesty, truth, and love, for which we can't form a clear mental image. Often, starting there and working your way up can be the most effective way.

PROPAGANDA

Don't underestimate the negative power of propaganda, which is defined as "information, ideas, or rumors deliberately spread widely to help or harm a person, group, movement, institution, nation, etc."[43] To "propagate" something means to actively promote it through various media such as books, tracts, blog articles, radio and television shows, and even the spoken word. Propaganda can be positive, negative, or neutral. But we're using the term "propaganda" here in its specifically negative sense. Historically, political propaganda has been a powerful tool for psychological suasion. We need only look at the Soviet Union, Mao's Communist China, North Korea, and, more recently, the sophisticated social media campaigns being waged by Al Qaeda and ISIS to see how effectively propaganda can be used to recruit, convince, and demoralize one's opponents.

Apologists have to deal with propaganda, too. The Jehovah's Witness publication mentioned above, *Should You*

Believe in the Trinity? is a prime example of propaganda. It isn't intended to simply explain what the Watchtower teaches about God. It's an all-out attack piece that mixes innuendo, historical fallacies, and out-of-context quotations to convince the reader that the Trinity is a confusing, unbiblical, and false Christian doctrine. *Should You Believe in the Trinity?* is especially destructive because its anti-Trinitarian screed does double duty by also attacking the divinity of Jesus Christ.

Other examples of religious (and antireligious) propaganda range from the lowbrow and lurid Chick Tracts, printed and distributed by the tens of millions by Fundamentalist Protestants, to the recent spate of atheist billboards urging people to abandon their belief in God.

The key here is to realize that apologetics may at times require your "deprogramming" someone who has become convinced by propaganda. Often, this can be accomplished by simply dismantling each false or semifalse claim by demonstrating its error, though this requires persistence and patient effort. Luckily, we live in the era of Google, so it's far easier to research things today than it ever was for any previous generation of apologists!

PEER PRESSURE

Peer pressure can be a significant, though not insurmountable, obstacle for someone who might otherwise believe and embrace the truth. Exerted by friends, coworkers, fellow parishioners, and especially family members, it can be extremely potent. Of course, peer pressure can be positive as well as negative. But often, in apologetics situations, negative peer pressure can inhibit someone's progress toward the truth. It pays, therefore, to remind the person you're dealing with that he or she should strive for the truth regardless of what others might say or do. Two examples of this come to mind, one that had a happy ending and one that didn't.

The first example involved an Evangelical Protestant whom I'll call "Tom." He called me one day and explained that he was "kind of" on the journey into the Catholic Church, though he still had many questions and objections. Tom felt deeply drawn to Catholicism, but wasn't sure if he was ready, willing, and able to go all the way. To greatly complicate matters, his wife, who was also a devout Evangelical, had gotten quite angry when she discovered his secret stash of Catholic books and websites bookmarked on his Internet browser.

"If you become Catholic," she told him angrily, "I promise I'll divorce you and take the children with me. There's no way I will stay married to a Catholic." Talk about *negative* peer pressure!

Fearful that he would lose his wife and kids, Tom would only call me when he was away from the house or she was out running errands. After a couple of conversations, I suggested that I send him a "care package" of Catholic apologetics books and CDs to help him study further, including my book *Surprised by Truth*, a collection of conversion testimonies by former Protestants who became Catholic.

"Okay," he said, "but you've *got* to make sure you send it in a plain package with no indication that it's from a Catholic organization. If my wife sees anything Catholic show up, she'll freak out."

"Not a problem," I assured him. And I sent the package off as completely nondescript as possible.

But a really big problem occurred. When the package arrived, Tom was out on an errand and couldn't intercept it. Tom's wife answered the door and received the oh-so-nondescript package addressed to her husband. When Tom returned, he was stunned to find his wife locked in their bedroom, screaming angrily that she was leaving him for good. Her curiosity had gotten the better of her, and she opened the box to see what it contained.

Tom slept on the couch that night, miserable and fearful of what would happen when dawn came. To his great surprise, in the early morning hours, his wife slipped out of the bedroom and came to where he was sleeping, shook him gently awake, and apologized to him tearfully for her furious behavior the night before. Kneeling beside the couch, she told him she wasn't angry. She said that she now understood more clearly why he might be interested in the Catholic Church and that she wouldn't stand in his way if that's where his heart was leading him.

Dumfounded, Tom asked her what had happened to change her mind about the Catholic Church so dramatically. She explained that when she opened the box and saw its contents, she became enraged and locked herself in the bedroom. After a while, she realized that she had locked herself in the bedroom *with the box* of books and CDs. So, bored and with nothing else to do, she started reading *Surprised by Truth*. Although at first very irritated by the message of the book, she soon became engrossed in the heartfelt stories. As she read her way through each chapter, she found her own misconceptions and objections to the Catholic Church being answered and cleared away.

The happy ending? Not only did Tom enroll in RCIA classes and become Catholic, but soon after, his wife *and their kids* also became Catholic. All because of the "bad luck" of a nondescript box arriving at his house at exactly the wrong (right) time.

The second story, I'm sorry to say, did not end happily. And peer pressure was to blame. I was taking some additional philosophy courses at a local college, and one of my professors, a middle-aged man whom I'll call Dr. Kraft, was a devout Mormon. Being an apologetics aficionado of Mormonism myself, you can imagine how happy I was to make this discovery.

I struck up a kind of friendship with Dr. Kraft outside the classroom, and we had many fascinating discussions about philosophy, God, and religion. He was very happy to tell me about his Mormon beliefs and seemed just as happy for me to tell him about my Catholic ones. At the end of the fall semester, I decided to give him a copy of Frank Sheed's *Theology and Sanity* as a Christmas gift. I knew he'd enjoy the deep and deeply logical way that Sheed explained the Faith, especially the Trinity, a doctrine that Dr. Kraft, as a Mormon, did not believe in. He happily accepted the gift and promised to read it with interest.

True to his word, when I visited Dr. Kraft's home a few weeks later for another discussion, I asked him if he had had a chance to read the book and whether he liked it. "Yes, indeed!" he said. "I not only read it, cover to cover, but I really enjoyed it *and* I thank you because I think I now finally understand clearly what you Catholics mean when you say "one God in Three Persons." I had never really understood that before, because it always seemed so contradictory to me. But now it makes sense, and I have to admit that I think the author, Sheed, is right about this."

Now I was dumbfounded. The prospect of Dr. Kraft becoming Catholic didn't seem so far-fetched now as I would have thought earlier. But my elation quickly evaporated as he explained why, even though the doctrine now made complete sense to him, he could never leave the Mormon Church.

"If I left, I would lose my wife, and my children would also turn against me. They're all devout members of the church. I'd lose my position at our local ward [similar to a Catholic parish], I'd be ostracized by my friends and family, and I'd be an outcast in the local LDS community. There's just no way.

This saddened me, but there was no way for me to argue against it. His emotions were deeply bound up in the positive peer pressure exerted on him by his loving wife and family, LDS friends, and members of his local LDS congregation. And conversely, opening himself up to the potential of the devastating *negative* peer pressure he would no doubt face if he became Catholic was simply too much for him to even contemplate.

To conclude this section, just remember that peer pressure can be powerful, yes, but the beauty of the truth and the gravitational pull of God's grace is far more powerful, at least for those who are willing to take the risk of giving up everything for that "pearl of great price." Some people are willing, and some, like Dr. Kraft, are not. But be persistent and patient and say lots of prayers for the person you're doing apologetics with that God would grant him or her the courage to let the truth "carry you where you do not wish to go" (John 21:18).

CHAPTER 6

Natural Apologetics
Making the Case for the Existence of God

"Natural apologetics," as the term suggests, involves an appeal to the natural world — the cosmos and everything in it — as the *prima facie* evidence for God's existence. St. Paul emphasized this truth saying:

> What can be known about God is plain to them, because God has shown it to them. Ever since the creation of the world his invisible nature, namely, his eternal power and deity, has been clearly perceived in the things that have been made. So they are without excuse. (Romans 1:19–20)

Nature itself reveals God to us. And it makes the case that God exists based solely on natural revelation. There is no need, at this level of apologetics, to invoke divine revelation (i.e., the Bible or Apostolic Tradition). For one reason, it would be pointless to do so when engaging someone who doesn't believe there's a "divine" anything out there anyway, much less that he/it has provided any revelation. Another reason is that nature itself is more than sufficient for providing us with solid, rational evidence that God exists. And the beauty about it is that one can do natural apologetics at the level of pure reason, without the need of faith in anything beyond what rational inquiry can tell us. Whether you're dealing with skeptics, agnostics, or atheists, you can rely solely on reason to make your case.

Now, more than at any time in Christian history, apologists must be equipped and prepared to defend their belief in God's existence. We are facing the ever-intensifying onslaught of atheist challenges on the airwaves, on the Internet, in books, in billboard campaigns, in court cases, and, of course, in person. The presence of atheist arguments against God's existence is no longer confined to the philosophy classrooms and faculty lounges of academia, a few hardly read atheist books, or the musings of the occasional atheist guest on late-night radio or television shows.

Today atheism has taken on a kind of religious fervor and ideological militancy that would do religious zealots proud. The atheistic, secular worldview has permeated nearly every level of American and European society. Books by popular God-deniers such as Richard Dawkins, Sam Harris, Daniel Dennett, and the late Christopher Hitchens become international best sellers very quickly. Hundreds of thousands, even millions, hang on every word that proceeds from their mouths via blog posts and YouTube videos.

Over the years that I've been doing apologetics it has become clear that countless parents of young adults are deeply worried by the fact that their sons and daughters have lost not just their Christian beliefs but their belief in God altogether. The pervasive atheist worldview on college campuses and its, at least superficially, persuasive case against the existence of God has duped them. These parents want to know what they can do, how they can talk to their sons and daughters, and how they can not only answer their doubts about God's existence, but also win them back to the truth. Using the arguments, tools, and techniques I'll outline in this chapter, anyone who wants to undertake that important mission is likely to meet with success in making a persuasive case for God.

Many Christians nowadays feel cowed by the new atheists, but there's no reason for this. We have the better arguments on our side. And those who engage in apologetics with atheists have the privilege of being able to present those arguments to an audience under stress.

The anti-God arguments raised by prominent atheists writers (e.g., Harris, Hitchens, Dawkins, and Dennett) generally fall into two major categories: scientific and philosophical, with the majority being appeals to science.

The first fact to realize about atheism is that, not only can science not prove the existence of God, science cannot *disprove* the existence of God. At best, applying the scientific method to God-related issues such as prayer, miracles, and the afterlife can only study and measure phenomena associated with such things and attempt to calculate probabilities.[44] One such study was conducted by University of Utah neuroscientists Julie Korenberg and Jeff Anderson, who used state-of-the-art medical equipment to scan people's brains in an effort to "capture what goes on in the brain of a believer during a religious moment."[45] Such medical tests are not new. But no matter how rigorously our scientific tools may be able to study human physiology, science cannot measure the supernatural.

Any time an atheist claims to "prove" God doesn't exist by some scientific inquiry, he shows how fundamentally he misunderstands the limits of science and the nature of the supernatural. Even so, to whatever extent science can shed light on how the supernatural affects the natural order, there is no conflict between science and faith in God.

Peter Kreeft and Fr. Ronald Tacelli list twenty discrete arguments for the existence of God in their masterwork, *Handbook of Catholic Apologetics*.[46] If you master just seven of them, you'll be more than prepared to hold your own in an apologetics discussion with an atheist or agnostic. The first five demonstrations of the reasonableness of faith were pioneered by Aristotle and refined by St. Thomas Aquinas. Each of these demonstrations relies purely on natural reason, unaided by grace, to arrive at the certitude not just that God exists, but that God must exist. For if, as we shall see, he does not exist, then there is no rational way to account for the universe and all that is in it.

Before we consider the first five arguments, classic formulations also known as "proofs for God's existence," let's first examine the concept of *intentionality*, which we see everywhere in the universe. Randomness and chaos are the opposite of intentionality. Imagine a strong earthquake shaking a hundred cans of different colored paint off the store shelf and onto the floor. The result would be a multicolor mess, but one that is totally random. There would be no intentional pattern for the way the paints landed and mixed together. It would be pure chaos. But if a painter used those same paints to create a huge floor mural of the solar system, for example, you would instantly see the difference. The mural painted by the painter would show evidence that the artist had a *goal* in mind. He wanted to depict the planets with their individual colors and unique orbits around the sun.

A related word to describe intentionality is *teleological*, which means the purpose for which a thing is made, the goal or end to which it tends. Simple examples include the eye and ear. The goal or end of the former is to see, and that of the latter is to hear. The teleology of an acorn is to become an oak tree. A pencil's is to write or draw. A handsaw's is to cut things. And an automobile's is to drive on the open road. Some things can have multiple uses, such as the brain, though even those uses have a unified purpose. In the case of the brain, it performs many functions, but all of them together are ordered toward the single goal of maintaining the health and well-being of the body.

When doing apologetics with atheists and agnostics, it can be very effective to explain the following proofs or evidences for God's existence without naming them. Quite often, the atheist will never have encountered these arguments and will not know them by their formal titles. So the more you can simply discuss the issue in a matter-of-fact way, walking him through each step of your logic, the more likely you are to get a fair hearing and to get the other guy to really start thinking about the truths these logical explanations point toward.

What follows here is how I might explain each of these arguments in favor of God's existence as if I were having a friendly discussion over a cup of coffee with an atheist. You can paraphrase these explanations in your own words, adding more or less detail, depending on the situation you're in. The more clearly these concepts are embedded in your own mind, the easier it will be for you to share them with others in a natural and confident way.

When doing apologetics, make your own analogies and any free-association comments and observations you might want to throw into the mix. Here is how I explain them:

MOTION AND CHANGE

Everything, no matter how large or small, is moving and changing, even down to the atomic level or up to the level of the universe itself. We can speak about "motion" in two ways: locomotion, in which an object moves from point A to point B through space; and change, in which a being rises from a state of potency to the state of act. That last bit is a more technical way of expressing change using Aristotelean metaphysical terms. "Potency" refers to the latent state of potentiality in which a thing *could* change in a particular way but has not yet changed (it might never change in that way, but it could).

"Act" is the state of the thing once it has changed. For example, this pencil in my hand *could* be broken in half. It's whole and unbroken right now, but it has the potential to change by being broken in two. When I snap the pencil in half, it has "risen from potency to act." The drinking glass on the table is empty, but it could be filled with water. It has the potential to be full of water but is not full yet, and maybe it will never be full. That's one type of transition from potency to act. Another is the result of time and how things age, moving from younger to older. It involves real change in a succession of moments, from the past, in the present, and moving into the future. Aristotle defined time as: "the numbering of motion according to before and after."[47]

Imagine you're about to play a game of billiards. You rack the balls and place them carefully on the white dot and move to the other end of the table with your cue stick to take the first shot. But suddenly, before you could do anything, all the balls started moving all over the table, totally without your having moved them by shooting the cue ball. Chances are, you'd skedaddle in fear because billiard balls are not supposed to move on their own without some outside force to move them (like the cue ball, gravity, or someone rolling them). The fact that they are moving through space from point A to point B is utterly inexplicable without some force causing that movement. As Peter Kreeft and Fr. Ronald Tacelli explain:

> Nothing can give itself what it does not have, and the changing thing cannot have now, already, what it will come to have then. The *result* of change cannot actually exist *before* the change. The changing thing begins with only the potential to change, but it needs to be acted on by other things outside if that potential is to be made actual. Otherwise, it cannot change. Nothing changes itself. Apparently self-moving things, like animal bodies, are moved by desire or will — something other than mere molecules. And when the animal or human dies, the molecules remain, but the body no longer moves because the desire or will is no longer present to move it.[48]

But notice that this universe is filled with countless moving, changing things, each of which requires something outside of itself to cause it to change and move. Remember the billiard balls: they cannot account for their own movement apart from some external force that sets them in motion. Indeed, the universe itself is moving and changing[49] — expanding rapidly, many astrophysicists say, and aging — so it too must have something *outside it*, acting upon it, to cause it to move and change. There is no rational way to explain how the entire cosmos and all its moving parts can all be moving and changing without something that initiated the motion, something outside this grand cosmic system that set all of it in motion. This thing, this being, must itself be unchangeable and immovable, an "unchanging changer" and an "unmoved mover."

Some philosophers refer to this being as the *prime mover,* meaning first mover. This being we call God.

THE PROOF FROM TIME AND CONTINGENCY

To be contingent means to be "unnecessary." No one likes to think of himself as unnecessary, but in fact, each of us and everything else in the universe[50] — indeed the universe itself — is unnecessary. No thing in the universe *must* exist, and the easiest way to prove this is that every thing in the universe at one time did not exist.

If something didn't exist at some point in the past, and if it will eventually go out of existence, then it does not necessarily exist (that is, nonbeing). And yet, we can see that, over time, countless things do come into and go out of existence. They all have being. The implications of this fact follow inexorably.

First, as we've seen, since nothing can give itself what it does not already have, nothing can give itself existence before it exists. Things cannot just "pop into existence," go from nonbeing into being. There is no "thing" there to start existing. Indeed, whatever exists received its existence from something preceding it in time.

Second, everything in the universe — galaxies, solar systems, stars, and planets, and everything on them and in them — came into existence *after* the universe did. You could say that, directly or indirectly, they received their existence from the universe. Fine. But the universe itself also came into existence. Which means ... since nothing can come from nothing ... something or Someone had to bring the universe into existence.

Third, since nothing in the universe can account for its own existence, including the universe itself, there is no way to rationally account for the existence of anything in the universe of time and space without there existing a being that is absolutely necessary, self-existent, and from which all existence flows. This being must be existence itself, and this being we call God.

EFFICIENT CAUSALITY

Imagine stopping at a train-track crossing. You arrive just in time to see the last few cars of the train pass in front of you, trailed at the very end by a caboose.

"Why is that caboose moving forward on the tracks?" your three-year-old daughter asks you. "Does it have an engine?"

"No, it doesn't have an engine, it moves because it's connected to the train car in front of it that's pulling it forward."

"Oh, well does *that* train car have an engine?" she asks.

And you explain that each train car can only move because the car ahead of it is pulling it. And at the head of that long line of cars you'll find the train's locomotive engine. It is moving under its own steam, so to speak, and it causes all the other cars behind it to move. Without its presence, though, none of the other cars could move, that is, they can't move on their own.

The locomotive is the *efficient cause* of the motion all the other cars have. In the same way, everything in the universe has a cause that effected its being brought into existence. Cars are brought into existence at car manufacturing plants. Trees are brought into existence from trees living before them whose seeds they sprang from. This book you're reading was brought into physical existence at the printing plant where it was printed and bound. And the words and concepts represented by the ink squiggles on the page sprang from the author's mind. The printer was the efficient cause of the physical artifact you call a book, and the author was the efficient cause of the ideas imparted to you in that artifact. The book didn't cause itself. You, yourself, the one reading the book, were caused by the physical union of your parents, just as they were caused by their parents, and so on. So, since nothing can be its own cause, its own source, and everything relies on something else to cause it, there must be a being that is an uncaused cause of all other things. That being we call God.

THE PROOF FROM DEGREES OF PERFECTION

You can tell when a line is crooked because you contrast it to the ideal of a perfectly straight line. Ditto for a wobbly circle. You know it's not a perfect circle only because you have in your mind the concept or standard of a perfect circle. Everything we experience in life is measured in terms of how close or how far it is on a spectrum with perfection at one end and imperfection at the other.

We identify things as good, better, best; bad, worse, worst; tall, taller, tallest; close, closer; closest; far, farther, farthest; some, more, most; pretty, prettier, prettiest; sweet, sweeter, sweetest; dark, darker, darkest, et cetera. These are known as degrees of perfection. But the only way something can be less than perfect is if there is something else that actually is perfect to which the first thing can be compared and contrasted.

Certain perfections cannot be seen or touched, but we know they are real nonetheless; for example, beauty, truth, goodness, love, et cetera. We value and are drawn to these things in art, in nature, and as qualities in other people. And yet, we know that even the most spectacularly dazzling sunset or majestic mountain or beautiful woman is not *perfect*. We all intuit at a deep level that there is something more perfect somewhere "out there," a perfect kind of beauty we only catch glimpses of here on earth.

We also know that no matter how beautiful or how good something or someone may be, even still, things and people are insufficient to fill that deep desire within us to obtain to that which is perfectly beautiful and perfectly good. We yearn for that absolute standard that alone can satisfy but which is never actually encountered in the people and things we experience day to day. This deep yearning for this ethereal perfection is real, and we should ask ourselves why we should even experience it.

Kreeft and Tacelli add a further precision:

> Sometimes it is the literal distance from an extreme that makes all the difference between "more" and "less." For example, things are more or less hot when they are more or less distant from a source of heat. The source communicates to those things the quality of heat they possess in greater or lesser measure. This means that the degree of heat they possess is caused by a source outside of them…. [Therefore] if these degrees of perfection pertain to being [i.e., existence], and being is *caused* in finite creatures, then there must be a "best," a source and real standard of all the perfections that we recognize belong to us *as beings*.[51]

This inexorable logic leads us to the realization that these degrees of perfection are predicated upon and pointing us toward a being that in itself possesses absolutely and without limit the plentitude of all perfections. That being we call God.

THE PROOF FROM DESIGN

First, note that this argument is distinct from what's popularly known as the "Intelligent Design" argument, sometimes employed in scientific discussions about creation. The argument from design does *not* seek to argue for any specific scientific conclusions as such. But, rather, it's a process of rational deduction to its reasonable conclusion: that God exists.[52]

The first premise is that the universe and all its constituent parts, however large or small, are highly complex and intricately ordered. By way of repeated observation and experiments that have never been contradicted, we perceive countless "laws of nature" that govern the natural order. Some are universal and absolute (e.g., the principles of conservation of mass-energy, momentum, and electrical charge).

These laws regulate everything from the motions of galaxies and the orbits of planets to the bonding of molecules. The growth and function of the human body, with all of its intricate systems and subsystems, is very clearly coordinated by a precise and consistent set of laws.

Sickness due to pathology is the result of those laws not being followed. In other words, everywhere we look, we see order and design, and we rightly wonder why. *Why* is there such staggering order and consistency at every level of this complex system we call the universe? Why not just randomness and chaos? Especially, why not chaos in a universe that atheists insist is meaningless? There are two possible answers to these questions.

First, the universe and all its parts are just the byproduct of eons of random, meaningless, chaotic forces working against one another and yet, somehow, out of that chaos, countless orderly systems governed by laws of nature have emerged. How that happened, we can't explain, but it's there, so we know it did happen.

Or second, there is a rational being who exists outside the universe, outside time-space, who imposed order upon the elements and organized them into a coherent, intentional design.

This second conclusion is a more reasonable way of accounting for the design we see all around us. The eye, for example, is clearly designed for a single purpose — to see. It is intentional in its very structure. It is goal-oriented. It is designed to accomplish a task. Things that are designed must have a designer.

Simple examples of this common-sense principle are endless: This book you hold in your hands carries in itself all the marks of being designed. Not just the meaning of the words on each page, which come from the mind that composed them, but the words themselves, the pages, the cover design, the binding, et cetera, all show quite clearly that the book was designed.

If someone were to try to convince you that the book you're holding was simply the happenstance result of eons of random, blind, natural forces acting against one another until finally, the book appeared in its present form, complete with order and meaning, you would laugh and walk away, and rightly so. As even small children can immediately intuit, something that *has meaning* cannot spring forth from a background of random meaninglessness.

As we've already seen, things don't come from nothing, and things cannot give themselves something they don't have in the first place. It takes a designer to impose order and meaning on chaos, or all there would be is chaos. Even in a million, billion lifetimes, a cherry red Ferrari will never be the result of a million billion tornadoes hitting a million billion junkyards. Random chance producing something so complex, intentional, and clearly designed as a high-performance motorcar is simply impossible. And the human body is far more complex, far more intentional, and far more clearly designed than any motorcar.

When doing apologetics with those who deny God's existence, it's helpful to appeal to their own everyday experience with things that everyone will recognize cannot be accounted for unless someone designed it. An iPhone, a shoe, a fork, an airplane, a clock, a freeway, a mini-market, a chair — starting with commonplace examples such as these, you can effectively prepare the other person's mind to think through the logical implications of this and the other classic rational arguments for God's existence.

In this effort, don't be afraid of science or of scientific discoveries. They in no way conflict with the belief that God exists; these findings actually bolster, rather than weaken, the case for God. The philosopher-scientist Fr. Robert J. Spitzer, S.J., is renowned for skillfully laying out the massive amount of new information science has provided for us that, far from disproving God's existence, actually points inexorably toward it. His superb book, *New Proofs for the Existence of God: Contributions of Contemporary Physics and Philosophy*,[53] delves deeply into these findings, showing that if God did not exist, there would simply be no logical, rational way to explain the evidences for design and intentionality inherent in these scientific findings.

Christian apologist Roy Williams takes it further by showing the difference between the "how" of the universe and the "why" of the universe as it relates to evaluating the argument for God's existence on the basis of evidence of design (that would require a Designer) literally everywhere in the universe:

> This dichotomy between the "how" and the "why" … seems to me to be a critical one to recognize…. When atheists like Richard Dawkins make large claims about the ambit of scientific knowledge, they can be talking — *at most* — about the "how" of the universe, not the "why." Often, their claims about the "how" are exaggerated. In general, these exaggerations fall into two categories. The first is the presentation of inference and opinion as scientific "fact." In *Letter to a Christian Nation*, Sam Harris declares bluntly that, "Nature offers no compelling evidence for an intelligent designer." That is an opinion, not a fact. There is a lot of evidence capable of leading a reasonable person to the very opposite opinion. Speaking for myself, the more I read of physics, chemistry, and biology, the more strongly I believe in God. The discoveries of science — and especially the more recent discoveries — point toward, rather than away from, God's existence. The universe is just too extraordinary to be a unique and happy accident.[54]

When doing apologetics, keep in mind that elaborating these arguments for the existence of God doesn't require complicated or highly technical explanations. The more you stick to the rules of sound logic and the more you clearly and methodically lay out the reasons why you believe what you believe, the more forthright and easy to grasp it will be. Remember, apologetics should never be about trying to "dazzle" the other person with a shock-and-awe display of your own knowledge and sophistication. Rather, let the truth do the dazzling. Truth is far more dazzling and breathtaking than even the cleverest argument made in its defense.

THE ARGUMENT FROM IMMATERIAL REALITIES

At the heart of the atheist worldview is the principle of naturalism (also known as "physicalism" and "scientism"). It holds that the only things that exist are natural, material, and thus susceptible to being studied, measured, and quantified by the scientific method using scientific instruments. Naturalism excludes the possibility of the existence of a supernatural realm. This means no God, no heaven and hell or spiritual afterlife of any sort, no angels and demons, and no human souls. This is a very useful weak point to exploit in any apologetics encounter with an atheist. I recommend the following steps:

First, establish with your atheist counterpart that he agrees with the premise of naturalism. If he doesn't agree, ask him how he explains the existence of a supernatural realm that is purely spiritual — that is, immaterial — if God does not exist. It's highly unlikely he will agree to follow this tack. Rather, he will almost certainly agree with the naturalist worldview.

Second, ask the atheist if you are correct in assuming that he believes nothing supernatural exists, only material things. He will very likely agree with this.

Third, ask him then how he can account for the existence of realities such as love, kindness, good and evil, honesty, human rights, memory, his own self-awareness as an individual person, and even truth itself given that all of these things he takes for granted in his day-to-day life are purely immaterial. One cannot produce a box of "truth" or a bag of "love," though we know these things do exist. They are not comprised of matter, so they exist in a realm that is above or at least apart from the material world. Let him think about this and do his best to explain them. Rigorously consistent atheists will recognize, and some will even admit that, if atheism is true and all that exists is material, then those concepts such as love, honesty, truth, and so on, really do not (in fact, cannot) exist apart from his own brain.

In my book with Kenneth Hensley, *The Godless Delusion: A Catholic Challenge to Modern Atheism*, we provide an extended explanation, including quotes from prominent atheist writers, showing that, to be logically consistent with naturalism, atheists inevitably must fall back to the position that love, et cetera, are really just the electrically charged chemical reactions taking place in the brain matter. Which, if true, leads to the following questions:

> 1. If these immaterial realities you think of as love, truth, et cetera, are really only physical reactions inside *your* brain matter, then how do you account for the fact that countless human beings everywhere and at all times have reached the exact same conclusions about them that you have?

> 2. If love, truth, et cetera, are not really independent of your own physiology but just biological byproducts of it, then how can you be certain you are not mistaken and they are not in fact real? Can you apply the scientific method or any scientific instrument to determine this?

> 3. If love, truth, et cetera, are really not immaterial, transcendent realities but are just

electrically charged chemical reactions in *my* own brain matter, then why should I bother with them? And if my belief in God is nothing more than the electrically charged chemical reactions in *my* brain matter, then why should it matter to you? Who cares? Why do you even bother to try and convince me that God doesn't exist? What does it matter?

Atheists live as if these things are real, transcendent things that exist apart from their own material physiologies. But their naturalist position really requires them to abandon that notion if they want to be consistent. Your job is to point out this curious lacuna in their thinking in hopes that they will recognize the irrational implications that flow from their position.

Simply put, the theistic word view can easily and reasonably account for these immaterial realities on the basis that God exists. But if atheists are correct and God does not exist, then it becomes exceedingly difficult to account for their existence. Press this point home, politely but firmly and vigorously. It's not likely that your doing so will result in the atheist having a sudden "Road-to-Damascus" conversion. But you *will* be planting the seeds of some very important intellectual conundrums he will have to think about perhaps long after your conversation has ended.

Remember that your job as an apologist is not to "get the sale" or "close the deal" then and there. Do the best you can, especially by asking these questions that, if honestly considered by atheists, lead to other questions and conclusions, all of which lie in the direction of accepting that God really does exist.

ETHICS AND MORALITY

This leads to the related issue of ethics and morality, a hot button issue for many atheists. Some atheists misunderstand the Christian argument that God must exist for good and evil and for any moral system to have any basis in reality. Many atheists wrongly assume that the Christian case for God's existence entails the notion that atheists cannot be "good people." This is, of course, not at all the case.

From a purely natural-virtue point of view,[55] yes, atheists can indeed be good, ethical people, and many are. So the first step here is to clearly explain that you are *not* saying that atheists cannot be moral. Admit right up front that, yes, some atheists are highly ethical and some are not (totalitarian Communist dictators come to mind as handy examples). Just so, some Catholics are highly ethical and some are not. At this level, you're dealing with a *human* issue, not a religious one.

The point you're aiming at here is the *why* of morality. *Why* should we do good and avoid evil if God doesn't exist and if this universe is simply a vast, purposeless collection of material things that come into and go out of existence with no goal and for no reason?

If the Darwinian model of evolution is in fact true and God does not exist, then we all have our own personal notions of what is right and wrong, good and evil. But if these are simply our own individual beliefs and nothing more, then they are purely subjective. In *that* kind of world, it would make perfect logical sense to say, "That may be true for you, but it's not true for me." If that logic were applied to any behavior (sexual, financial, aggressive, deceptive, etc.) in a world where God does not exist, it would make sense. But we all know that some things are good (e.g., honesty, beauty, love, truth) and some things are evil (murder, lying, cheating, stealing) whether anyone agrees or not. These values transcend our own individual, subjective tastes and preferences. So, the approach to take when doing apologetics in this area is to affirm the existence of God on the basis that we all recognize instinctively that such a moral code does exist. And we should argue that there is no rational way to claim it *should* exist, much less that anyone should bother to feel obligated to adhere to it, if God does not exist. Yes, atheists can be moral people, but there is no compelling *transcendent* reason why they should do so if God does not exist. Why not simply get what you can get from whomever you can for as long as you can? Keep asking these questions and probe for the answers.

THE PROBLEM OF EVIL

Of all the varied atheist arguments against God's existence, this is by far the most formidable because it gets right to the heart of a singular mystery we all experience and puzzle over. What follows is a short-form explanation of the problem of evil argument and two ways to demonstrate that it must presuppose God's existence in order to make any rational sense. Kreeft and Tacelli explain:

> [T]he problem of evil is uniquely important … because it is universal. Everyone wonders why bad things happen to good people; some wonder why bad things happen at all. Incidentally, this very wonder hints at a solution to the problem of evil. The fact that we do not naturally accept this world full of injustice, suffering, sin, disease and death, the very fact of our outrage at evil is a clue that we are in touch

with a standard of goodness by which we judge this world as defective, as falling drastically short of the mark…. The problem of evil is not merely a theoretical problem but an intensely practical one.[56]

The early Christian writer Lactantius (A.D. 250–325) responded to the rendition of the "problem of evil" argument raised by the pagan Greek philosopher Epicurus (341–270 B.C.) by parsing out the problem in its fullest form:

> "God," he says, "either wants to eliminate bad things and cannot, or can but does not want to, or neither wishes to nor can, or both wants to and can.
>
> "If he wants to and cannot, then he is weak and this does not apply to god.
>
> "If he can but does not want to, then he is spiteful which is equally foreign to god's nature.
>
> "If he neither wants to nor can, he is both weak and spiteful, and so not a god.
>
> "If he wants to and can, which is the only thing fitting for a god, where then do bad things come from? Or why does he not eliminate them?"[57]

St. Thomas Aquinas expressed the problem of evil like this:

> If one of two contraries is infinite, the other is completely destroyed.
>
> But "God" means infinite goodness.

If, therefore, God existed, there would be no evil discoverable in the world.

But there is evil.

Therefore God does not exist.[58]

Famed Christian apologist C. S. Lewis expressed it like this in his book *The Problem of Pain*:

If God is all-good, he wants his creatures to be happy.

And if he is all-powerful, he can do whatever he wants.

But the creatures are not happy.

Therefore God lacks either goodness or power or both.[59]

The conclusion atheists reach is that, because evil does exist, God cannot exist. Simple enough. But as we saw earlier, the very dilemma itself pivots on the question of how can we rationally speak of "evil" if there is no ultimate standard of good against which we can contrast it? In other words, God.

The first step in answering the atheist view is to point out that "evil" is not a thing or a substance. Rather, evil is the privation of a due good the way blindness is a privation of sight and deafness is the absence of hearing. It's a privation of something that should be there but is not.

Also, evil is not something God created but is in fact the result of human freedom run amok by choosing against God's commandments. Adam and Eve started the terrible catastrophe of sin in motion by their original sin of disobeying God. Untold negative consequences for them and all their descendants, including you and me, rippled outward from that act. "Human beings cause moral evils, such as hatred, killing, lying, and stealing. Notice, though, that even though God is all-powerful, he is incapable of doing anything contradictory to his own divine nature. The key example of this is that he created human beings with free will.

Because God respects our freedom and "runs the risk" of our freely choosing against rather than for him, he permits our evil actions to run their natural course of hardship and pain. Though he does not *cause* evil, he nonetheless permits it out of respect for our freedom, and he even brings good out of evil.

Lastly, it is true that we often cannot see why a good and loving God would permit such pain and suffering that flows from evil if he truly loved us. There is the rub. The answer to that question remains to some extent out of our reach because we can't see this larger meaning in this life, with all its suffering, from an eternal perspective.

Much like the little child who, when taken to the emergency room to have a deep wound cleaned and stitched up, cannot understand why her mommy and daddy allow the doctor to inflict pain on her and why they don't do anything to step in and stop it. Why they just stand there and let her suffer as the doctor is doing his work. Later, when she's old enough, she'll understand that they were allowing that pain to happen out of love for her.

NATURAL DISASTERS

Atheists also significantly point to natural disasters as an objection to a God who is supposed to be all-good. Robert B. White, in his book *Who Is to Blame?*,[60] offers the best response to this objection. Here are the main elements of his argument:

1. God created a consistent, orderly world, complete with volcanoes, floods, and earthquakes, which he pronounced as "very good."

2. Many of the processes that make it possible for humans to live on earth are the same as those that give rise to disasters. Without volcanoes and earthquakes, for example, the earth would be largely a frozen flatland that could not support life.

3. Natural disasters don't cause the deaths attributed to them. Human beings do. Ninety-five percent of the deaths occurring from volcanoes, floods, and earthquakes can be blamed on humans not properly caring for the earth and her people. For example, most deaths from earthquakes come from buildings collapsing because they were not built to code. And from floods because governments fail to make and enforce evacuation plans.

4. Humans rebelled against God, thus breaking a close relationship with him and with the created, natural order. As a consequence we live in a broken world that cries out for restoration, which will occur when Jesus returns and brings to fulfillment the new creation.

5. In the meantime, we are called to work on the earth in line with God's priorities so that his will may be done on earth as it is in heaven.

We must remember, White says, that "Christianity can speak into the problem of suffering and evil with more certainty, with more hopefulness, with more conviction that in the fullness of time justice and righteousness" will prevail than can any secular source.[61]

PASCAL'S WAGER

Lastly, we'll conclude this chapter by briefly considering "Pascal's Wager" as another way of arguing for God's existence.[62] It's not so much a proof for his existence as a compelling reason to bet that he does and then live accordingly. Pascal's Wager is expressed this way in the *Catholic Encyclopedia*:

> God exists or He does not exist, and we must of necessity lay odds for or against Him.
>
> If I wager *for* and God is — infinite gain [heaven];
>
> If I wager *for* and God is *not* — no loss [no hell].
>
> If I wager *against* and God *is* — infinite loss [hell];
>
> If I wager *against* and God is *not* — neither loss nor gain [no heaven, no hell].[63]

Pascal's point here, which you should present to your atheist counterpart for his consideration, is that the "smart money" bets on God's existence. Why? Because if you believe in him, and live accordingly, you will go to heaven. You've lost nothing, except for perhaps a bit of immoral "fun" in this brief earthly life. But you gain an eternity of happiness.

If you believe in him and he does not exist, you've lost nothing, except perhaps a bit of immoral "fun" in this life.

If you don't believe in him and he doesn't exist, you've gained a little in the way of a bit of fun (which we couldn't properly call "immoral," even if those stuffy religious types do), and you get nothing but nothingness when you die.

And if you don't believe in him and he *does* exist, you lose everything because you spend eternity suffering the pain of separation from God. Nothing could be worse.

CHAPTER 7

Christian Apologetics
Making the Case for Jesus Christ

Just as demonstrating the reasonableness of theism is to lay the *foundation* of Faith, demonstrating the reasonableness of Christianity is to build the ground floor upon which everything else will rest. The human intellect is capable of arriving at a certain knowledge that God exists and that he is a personal, good, and loving being. But that is as far as it can proceed on its own, unaided by divine revelation. This is where we venture into the realm of Christian apologetics.

The goal now, after showing why one should believe in God at all, is to show why one should believe that Jesus Christ is God incarnate. What are the rational proofs for this? What, in addition to nature itself, must we turn to for help? The answer: a combination of rational deductions and inductions on the basis of the historical and biblical data, as well as divine revelation. All three combine to form the substance of Christian apologetics. And to make a comprehensive, effective, and compelling case for Christianity, you must master at least the basics of these elements. You must know how to deploy them for maximum effect in your presentation of the reasons for faith.

If a skeptic objects to a specific aspect of Christianity — for example, the Resurrection — it's fine to begin your presentation of the facts there. But if you have the opportunity to "tell the whole story" in logical progression, I suggest you do it in the following sequence of five areas: Jesus as a historical person, Jesus' public ministry, Jesus' teachings, the Resurrection, the divinity of Christ, and what conclusions one should draw from these things. You want to build your arguments with a cumulative force toward that last part — the conclusions we should draw. When you reach that point, the case you've made, that Jesus is our Lord and Savior, should be sufficiently persuasive as to merit serious consideration and, hopefully, acceptance.

There are several excellent books that lay out the details of each of these five areas of evidence. All of them are listed in the resources section at the end of this book. Here I will only give you the overall pattern of how to make your apologetics case for Christ using the specific data you will find in those books.

JESUS AS A HISTORICAL PERSON

The logical place to begin is by answering the skeptic's question, "How can I know if Jesus ever even existed?" Maybe he is just a fictional character like Santa Claus. Maybe, whoever he may have been, he was not the mythical "God-Man" Christians worship and follow.

Maybe he was just a guy who had some good ideas, but that was all — but he never made any of the extravagant claims about himself or his teachings that his unscrupulous followers eventually started making after he died. Or maybe Jesus was, in fact, a profoundly charismatic and mystical teacher, guru, prophet, philosopher, leader, master, sage, or _____ (fill in the blank). But his philosophy got hijacked by those same unscrupulous followers who saw a way to make money, win friends, and influence people by spinning Jesus' teachings, like so much cotton candy, into an elaborate zig-gurat of dogmas, rules, and mystical (but false) claims about his divinity. These are some of the theories about who Jesus may have really been, if he had existed at all.[64]

It won't do much good to make the case for other aspects of Christianity if you haven't first demonstrated that its founder, Jesus, actually existed as a real historical figure. You must show that he lived at the time and in the place where the Gospels say he did.

I've found it helpful to volunteer to the skeptic that, for the time being, you do not rely on the New Testament as documentary evidence for your claim that Jesus really lived at a certain time and place. This does two things, both of which work to your advantage: First, you show good faith by being willing to go outside the biblical account for data that can corroborate your theses about Jesus. Second, you will actually strengthen the impact on the listener when it becomes clear that you do not need to appeal to the Bible to make a convincing case that Jesus existed as a real historical figure.[65]

The extant historical evidence establishes an irrefutable case that Jesus of Nazareth was born in Judea, almost certainly in either 3 or 2 B.C. You should cite first the examples of *hostile* witnesses to the existence of Jesus among both contemporary Roman pagan as well as Jewish authors. They had no reason to prop up a myth about Jesus because they were opposed to the spread of Christianity.[66]

Jewish sources that corroborate Jesus' existence, public ministry, death, and the advent of the Church include:

Flavius Josephus (A.D. 37–100), a prolific Jewish historian who was also well-acquainted with the Roman world. In his landmark work, *Antiquities of the Jews*, he writes:

About this time there lived Jesus, a wise man, if indeed one ought to call him a man. For he was one who performed surprising deeds and was a teacher of such people as accept the truth gladly. He won over many Jews and many of the Greeks. He was the Messiah. And when, upon the accusation of the principal men among us, Pilate had condemned him to a cross, those who had first come to love him did not cease. He appeared to them spending a third day restored to life, for the prophets of God had foretold these things and a thousand other marvels about him. And the tribe of the Christians, so called after him, has still to this day not disappeared. (*Antiquities of the Jews*, 18.3.3, 63)[67]

Pagan authors who were contemporaries of the Apostles or who lived shortly after the apostolic era (i.e., the close of the first century) wrote a variety of things that either directly or indirectly corroborate the existence of Jesus the Christ.[68]

Publius Cornelius Tacitus (A.D. 56–117) served as a senator in Imperial Rome and was also an important historian of antiquity. In his work the *Annals*, he writes:

[T]here were sacred banquets and nightly vigils [in Rome] celebrated by married women. But all human efforts, all the lavish gifts of the emperor, and the propitiations of the gods, did not banish the sinister belief that the conflagration [i.e., the fire that destroyed the city of Rome] was the result of an order [i.e., ordered by the Emperor Nero himself]. *Consequently, to get rid of the report, Nero fastened the guilt and inflicted the most exquisite tortures on a class hated for their abominations, called Christians by the populace. Christus, from whom the name had its origin, suffered the extreme penalty during the reign of Tiberius at the hands of one of our procurators, Pontius Pilatus, and a most mischievous superstition, thus checked for the moment, again broke out not only in Judaea, the first source of the evil, but even in Rome,* where all things hideous and shameful from every part of the world find their center and become popular.[69]

Pliny the Younger (A.D. 61–112) was a pagan Roman who, as governor of Bythinia in modern-day Turkey, penned an account of the Christian communities he investigated for the Roman Emperor Trajan. He describes certain Christians who, when caught up in the dragnet of persecution, apostatized and renounced Christ. These wretches also, he says, provided one of the earliest extrabiblical accounts of Christian morality and fellowship.[70]

Suetonius (A.D. 69–140), a renowned pagan Roman historian, wrote the following about Christ and Christians: "Because the Jews at Rome caused constant disturbances at the instigation of Chrestus [his misspelling of the Greek *Christos*], he [the Emperor] expelled them from the city" (*Life of Claudius*, 25:4). Also, "Nero inflicted punishment on the Christians, a sect given to a new and mischievous religious belief" (*Lives of the Caesars*, 26.2).

THE CLAIMS OF JESUS

Another important component in making the case for Christ is to demonstrate that, unlike the founders of other major religions (e.g., Moses, Zarathustra, Lao Tzu, Gautama Buddha, Confucius, and Muhammad), Jesus Christ made startling claims about his own identity, authority, and mission that are utterly unique. He claimed to be the Son of God (e.g., Matthew 11:27; Mark 14:61–62; John 5:25, 10:36, 11:4, 17:1), and he allowed others to call him the Son of God (e.g., Matthew 4:3–7, 16:15–17, John 1:49–50, 11:25–27). Many eyewitnesses who were present at his baptism in the River Jordan also saw the Holy Spirit descend over him. And they simultaneously heard the voice of God the Father speaking from heaven the words, "You are my beloved Son; with you I am well pleased" (Luke 3:21–22). His disciples also called him the Son of God and identified him as divine (John 1:1, 14, 18, 3:16–18, 20:31).

Most significantly, Jesus himself clearly and repeatedly claimed to be God. Just before commencing his public ministry, Jesus fasted in the desert for forty days and, when the devil came to tempt him with worldly blandishments, he rebuked him saying, "You shall not tempt Lord your God" (Matthew 4:7).

Consider these declarations of his divinity: "Jesus said to them [the Jewish leaders], "Truly, truly, I say to you, before Abraham was, I am" (John 8:58), whereupon the Jews "took up stones to throw at him" (John 8:59). He declared: "My sheep hear my voice, and I know them, and they follow me; and I give them eternal life, and they shall never perish, and no one shall snatch them out of my hand. My Father, who has given them to me, is greater than all, and no one is able to snatch them out of the Father's hand. I and the Father are one" (John 10:27–30, see also John 14:9). Again, "the Jews took up stones again to stone him. Jesus answered them, 'I have shown you many good works from the Father; for which of these do you stone me?' The

Jews answered him, 'We stone you for no good work but for blasphemy; because you, being a man, make yourself God'" (John 10:31–33, see also John 5:12).[71] When Jesus declared "I AM," he was using the Divine Name, and the Jews clearly understood what he meant. Notice that he did not try to correct their understanding.

In addition to claiming that he himself was God, Jesus also affirmed monotheism (hinting at the Trinity):

> And one of the scribes came up and heard them disputing with one another, and seeing that he answered them well, asked him, "Which commandment is the first of all?" Jesus answered, "The first is, 'Hear, O Israel: The Lord our God, the Lord is one; and you shall love the Lord your God with all your heart, and with all your soul, and with all your mind, and with all your strength.'" (Mark 12:28–30)

After his Resurrection, his apostles were even more clearly aware that Jesus is God. One of the Twelve Apostles, "Doubting" Thomas, fell to his knees and addressed him as "My Lord and my God!" (John 20:28). And even though the faith of some seemed to waver, we read this about the Apostles' reaction to Jesus' power and glory just before he ascended into heaven: "When they saw Him, they worshiped Him; but some doubted" (Matthew 28:17).

Finally, note that Jesus also claimed absolute exclusivity as necessary for salvation: "Jesus said to him, 'I am the way, and the truth, and the life; no one comes to the Father, but by me'" (John 14:6).

THE MIRACLES OF JESUS

It's one thing to claim authority, but it's something else altogether to back up those claims with stupendous miracles. One way Jesus got people's attention was to perform miracles that were so astounding, so mind-blowingly beyond anything they had experienced before, that they were forced to confront the question, not, "Who is he?" but *"What* is he?" The Four Gospels recount his numerous miracles, performed in the presence of many witnesses, not a few of whom were deeply skeptical of him. And some eagerly sought for opportunities to expose him as a fraud and a charlatan. But the skeptics were endlessly disappointed in this quest, for Jesus proved his own authenticity as the Son of God by his miracles.

He cured blindness, deafness, and disfiguring skin diseases like leprosy. He read the hidden secrets of many hearts, foretold the future, walked on water, walked through walls, and walked unharmed through hostile, angry mobs who tried to lay hands on him to kill him. He healed crippled and paralyzed people. He calmed storms with a word of command, cast out demons, caused a miraculous catch of fish, and multiplied a handful of loaves and fish to feed twenty thousand people. He transubstantiated water into wine, restored a severed ear, instantly converted hardened sinners, and raised people from the dead. Indeed, Jesus' entire three-year ministry was one long succession of startling, breathtaking miracles that confounded everyone and convinced many the he was the Son of God.

When you reach this part of your case for Christ be prepared for the skeptic to counter with something like, "Those are just stories. Just fables. Jesus didn't really perform those miracles; his disciples just exaggerated the good things he did."

One response to this objection is to ask, "How could that have possibly worked? After all, the apostolic authors wrote the four Gospels and most of the New Testament letters in the years and decades immediately following the events they described. Countless eyewitnesses (including the hostile Jewish authorities) to Jesus' public ministry were still alive. And before they wrote these events down, they preached them publically for years (see Luke 1:1–4). So, how is it that no one stepped forward and denounced Jesus' miracles as fictions? One would expect that at least *some* of them would have reared up and cried "fraud!" if the Apostles had concocted false stories. And yet, no one did. No one attempted to discredit the New Testament depiction of Jesus as a miracle-worker. We have plenty of literature from the first few centuries after Jesus. And they don't charge the Apostles with spreading fraudulent accounts of Jesus' miracles.

Furthermore, those who personally witnessed the miracles knew what they had seen and were willing to proclaim it, often in the face of severe "pushback" from the Jewish leaders and others who opposed Christianity and wanted to see it die. Later Jewish writers,[72] centuries after Christ, made mostly veiled references to Jesus as a worker of sorcery, though they didn't deny that his ministry was marked by astonishing deeds that Christians know to be miracles.

Jesus also showed his divine power by claiming to forgive sins, another aspect of his bold public preaching that shocked and agitated many religious leaders.

And they came, bringing to him a paralytic carried by four men. And when they could not get near him because of the crowd, they removed the roof above him; and when they had made an opening, they let down the pallet on which the paralytic lay. And when Jesus saw their faith, he said to the paralytic, "Child, your sins are forgiven." Now some of the scribes were sitting there, questioning in their hearts, "Why does this man speak like this? It is blasphemy! Who can forgive sins but God alone?" And immediately Jesus, perceiving in his spirit that they questioned like this within themselves, said to them, "Why do you question like this in your hearts? Which is easier, to say to the paralytic, 'Your sins are forgiven,' or to say, 'Rise, take up your pallet and walk'? But that you may know that the Son of man has authority on earth to forgive sins" — he said to the paralytic — "I say to you, rise, take up your pallet and go home."

And he rose, and immediately took up the pallet and went out before them all; so that they were all amazed and glorified God, saying, "We never saw anything like this!" (Mark 2:3–12)

Remember: The fact that the Gospels record that Jesus claimed the power to forgive sins and he claimed to be God is not going to impress, much less sway, non-Christian skeptics who do not accept the New Testament as inspired Scripture and therefore authoritative. But that's unimportant at this point in your case for Christ. Simply make note of the fact that the Gospels *make the claim* that Jesus performed miracles. This strengthens your hand because it presents another question to the skeptic: If Jesus really didn't perform all of the many amazing miracles his followers claim to have seen with their own eyes, and if his followers publicized these claims, then why is there such a loud silence about this from all their contemporaries who were opponents of Christianity? They would assuredly have pounced on any opportunity to refute and discredit the nascent religion.

THE RESURRECTION

In his first letter to the Corinthians, St. Paul lays out the high stakes involved with the Resurrection. If it's true, it proves that Jesus is divine, and if it's not true, it proves Jesus was just a man like us. Christianity would therefore be a sham. Meditate deeply on these words before you attempt to mount your apologetics explanation of the Resurrection:

> Now I would remind you, brethren, in what terms I preached to you the gospel, which you received, in which you stand, by which you are saved, if you hold it fast — unless you believed in vain.
>
> For I delivered to you as of first importance what I also received, that Christ died for our sins in accordance with the Scriptures, that he was buried, that he was raised on the third day in accordance with the Scriptures, and that he appeared to Cephas, then to the Twelve. Then he appeared to more than five hundred brethren at one time, most of whom are still alive, though some have fallen asleep. Then he appeared to James, then to all the apostles. Last of all, as to one untimely born, he appeared also to me. For I am the least of the apostles,

unfit to be called an apostle, because I persecuted the Church of God....

Now if Christ is preached as raised from
the dead, how can some of you say that there
is no resurrection of the dead? *But if there is
no resurrection of the dead, then Christ has not
been raised; if Christ has not been raised, then
our preaching is in vain and your faith is in
vain.* We are even found to be misrepresenting
God, because we testified of God that he raised
Christ, whom he did not raise if it is true that
the dead are not raised. For if the dead are not
raised, then Christ has not been raised.

*If Christ has not been raised, your faith is
futile and you are still in your sins. Then those
also who have fallen asleep in Christ have perished. If for this life only we have hoped in Christ,
we are of all men most to be pitied.*

But in fact Christ has been raised from the
dead, the first fruits of those who have fallen
asleep. For as by a man came death, by a man
has come also the resurrection of the dead. For
as in Adam all die, so also in Christ shall all be
made alive. (1 Corinthians 15:1–9; 12–21)

I recommend you start your defense of the Trinity
by reading this passage to your discussion counterpart. Explain that this is how serious you take this doctrine and that
you have solid, factual reasons for believing in the Resurrection. Also, be sure to define carefully what you mean by
the term "Resurrection" so that you don't give someone a
misimpression. By it we do *not* mean that Jesus was revived
or resuscitated after having a "near death experience." We

do not mean that Jesus only "rose again" as a pure spirit. We do not mean that Jesus was "raised from the dead" by some outside power. It wasn't a myth or a legend or an exaggerated tale told by a band of fear-addled disciples.[73]

What we *do* mean by the Resurrection is that Jesus, by his own power, rose from the dead in his glorified body. It wasn't a vision or a hallucination his disciples saw; he didn't appear as a ghost. If it's helpful at this juncture of the conversation, you might want to read this passage to show your discussion partner that the New Testament witnesses to the Resurrection saw and touched the Risen Jesus:

> As they were saying this, Jesus himself stood among them, and said to them, "Peace to you." But they were startled and frightened, and supposed that they saw a spirit. And he said to them, "Why are you troubled, and why do questionings rise in your hearts? See my hands and my feet, that it is I myself; handle me, and see; for a spirit has not flesh and bones as you see that I have." *And when he had said this, he showed them his hands and his feet.* And while they still disbelieved for joy, and wondered, he said to them, "Have you anything here to eat?" They gave him a piece of broiled fish, and he took it and ate before them. (Luke 24:36–43)

Here is a basic sketch of how I would lay out the case for the truth of the Resurrection, step by step:

> 1. Contemporary and near contemporary documentary sources — pagan, Jewish, and Christian — all concur that Jesus was put to death by crucifixion in the city of Jerusalem, Province

of Judea, by the Romans under the procuratorship of Pontius Pilate. This triangulation of corroboration makes a cogent defense for the historicity of the Crucifixion.

2. The Gospel accounts make it amply clear that Jesus was subjected to enormous trauma and pain as the result of his torturous ordeal leading up to the crucifixion: exhaustion from repeated interrogations; lack of food, water, and sleep; being physically assaulted by guards; mercilessly flogged with whips (think blood loss, tissue and nerve damage); crowned with thorns which were forcibly embedded into his scalp and cranial tissue (more shock, more blood loss); he was forced to carry a heavy wooden cross for the better part of a mile, holding it on his lacerated shoulders and back; the cloak he was wearing was torn suddenly from his body, pulling with it the dried blood and patches of torn skin and lacerated muscles that had adhered to the fabric; his hands and feet were nailed to the cross with large spikes; and he was exposed to the sun and elements for three hours before he died, dehydrated and famished.

When the Roman guards broke the legs of the two thieves crucified with Jesus, they did not break his legs, but instead, to ensure death had come, plunged a spear into the side of his chest, piercing his heart and lungs. Subsequently a large quantity of his blood and plasma gushed out of his chest cavity (i.e., he "bled out").

After he was taken down from the cross, his mother Mary and other holy women wrapped his lifeless body tightly in winding cloths for burial. He was finally interred in a recently hewn rock tomb, the entrance to which was sealed with a large, heavy stone that was rolled in place to close it.

As others have asked before, if Jesus didn't move the stone, if the Apostles (who were at that time a scattered band of frightened and desperate fugitives who were terrified that they too might be captured and killed) didn't move the stone; if the Roman soldiers were on the lookout for anyone who might attempt to steal Jesus' body, then ... who moved the stone?

3. The Apostles and the other disciples declared with no hesitation or uncertainty that Jesus rose from the dead. They even, when writing about this in the Gospels, went out of their way to include mention of the conspiracy theory that had been floated in an effort to explain away the fact that the Lord's body was not found in the tomb on Easter morning (e.g., that they had stolen his body and pretended he had risen).

4. There is no way that Jesus could have survived the Crucifixion given the drastic trauma inflicted on his body. The so-called "swoon theory," which posits that Jesus only appeared

to die but "came to" in the total darkness of the tomb; somehow extricated himself from the winding cloths; managed to locate the entrance in complete darkness; in his utterly devastated physical condition had the strength to roll away the heavy stone; and make his escape while not being noticed by the detachment of Roman soldiers who had been stationed immediately outside to guard the tomb, simply isn't plausible.

5. There were many eyewitnesses to Jesus after his Resurrection: 1 Peter 5:1, 2 Peter 1:16–17, 1 John 1:1–3, 1 Corinthians 15:5–8. All of them testified that they saw him, spoke to him, and many of them even touched him. The Apostles ate several meals with him.

6. The many witnesses to the Resurrection were willing to be harassed — some were tortured and even killed — for not wavering in their testimony that they had seen the resurrected Jesus. There is no way this could have been a mass hallucination or mass psychosis.

7. The Apostles and other disciples had nothing to gain from telling a lie about Jesus rising from the dead. They did not receive any of the emoluments liars are motivated by: they got no money, no social status or influence in society, no sexual favors from women. No, they got nothing but harassment; being hunted by the authorities; and, when they were caught, as many were, tortured to force a recantation

(none of them recanted their testimony), and then put to death. There is no way, humanly speaking that hundreds and even thousands of regular people would be willing to die for a lie.

8. The only plausible conclusion is that Jesus really did rise from the dead as he predicted he would. His life, his character, his rectitude, his profound and majestic teachings, and his miracles all point to his divinity. And his Resurrection was the final, ultimate proof of this. The classical "trilemma" of Jesus being either a liar, a lunatic, or Lord, can be resolved by an appeal to the above chain of evidence and logic. Jesus didn't "fit the psychological profile" of a liar. He preached the necessity of telling the truth. He was selfless, dedicated, kind, generous, and honest. Nor did he fit the profile of a lunatic. People didn't feel pity for him; they were drawn to him. Read the Gospels to see just how lucid and compelling he was and how coherent his teachings were. The only plausible option that adequately accounts for all of the above data is that Jesus really was who he said he was: God.

THE DIVINITY OF CHRIST

Now that you've made the case for Christ using all the preceding component parts, you've arrived at the conclusion: Jesus is God. The New Testament is exceedingly clear about this. John 1:1, 14, reads: "In the beginning was the Word [Christ], and the Word was with God, and the Word was God.... And the Word became flesh and dwelt among us, full of grace and truth; we have beheld his glory, glory as of the only-begotten Son from the Father." St. Paul echoed these words, saying that Jesus is "the image of the invisible God" (Colossians 1:15).

He "reflects the glory of God and bears the very stamp of his nature" (Hebrews 1:3).

Once you've established your rational, historical, and biblical case for this truth, it would be wise to transition from the evidence itself to your own convictions about what that evidence means. Share from the heart your own personal faith in Jesus as Lord and Savior, Messiah and Redeemer.

Explain in your own words why you have placed your faith in him. In doing apologetics, it's important, of course, to present as best you can the pertinent data. But all the data in the world, however important, will not be as effective in saving souls *by itself* as it will be when you weld to it your own testimony of faith in Christ. Explain why you believe Jesus is God and why that makes all the difference to you as a Catholic. Point out that if Jesus isn't divine, then Christianity is sham and your faith is in vain. Christianity stands or falls on whether Jesus is divine. If he is, then the only answer to mankind's most urgent problems and desires is to accept him as Lord and Savior, embrace his teachings, become his disciple, and enter into the Catholic Church he founded.

The Catholic Church, which preaches and teaches in his name (Luke 10:16, Matthew 18:18) and with his authority (Matthew 16:18, 28:18–20) is the ark of salvation given by Jesus for us. It's helpful to remind your listener at this point that, like Noah's Ark, the Catholic Church is a rambunctious, messy, and even at times difficult, place because it is a divine institution comprised of weak human members (i.e., you and me). But the Catholic Church is also the

Bride of Christ and contains within itself all the treasures of powerful goodness that her Bridegroom lavished upon her. To accept Jesus' divinity and acknowledge him as Lord and Savior necessarily entails entering the Church he established. As the old song says, "You can't have one without the other."

Kreeft and Tacelli summarize the importance of the case for Christ this way, which is a good way to conclude your own presentation of the case to a skeptic:

> If Christ is divine, then the incarnation, or "enfleshing" of God, is the most important event in history. It is the hinge of history. It changes everything. If Christ is God, then when he died on the cross, heaven's gate, closed by sin, opened up to us for the first time since Eden. No event in history could be more important to every person on earth than that.... [I]f Christ is God, then, since he is omnipotent and present right now, he can transform you and your life right now as nothing and no one else possibly can. He alone can fulfill the psalmist's desperate plea to "create in me a clean heart, O God" (Psalm 51:10). Only God can create;... And if Christ is divine, he has a right to our entire lives, including our inner life and our thoughts. If Christ is divine, our absolute obligation is to believe everything he says and obey everything he commands. If Christ is divine, the meaning of freedom becomes conformity to him.[74]

Finally, now that we've seen the outline of how to demonstrate the reasonableness of believing in the divinity of Christ, to complete your case for Christianity you must now also demonstrate why Christians believe in the Trinity: One God in three Divine Persons. Granted, this is difficult territory because this sublime truth is so far beyond our limited human capacity to understand that we call it, and rightly so, a *mystery.* But remember that, as many Catholic saints and doctors have pointed out, a mystery such as the Trinity is not something one can know *nothing* about; a mystery is something one cannot know *everything* about.

When making the case for the Trinity, bear in mind who your audience is. If you're speaking to a Jehovah's Witness (who explicitly denies the Trinity and the divinity of Christ), it's important to focus on the biblical evidence. If you're speaking to a Mormon (whose Church teaches that though there is a "Godhead" of Father, Son, and Holy Ghost, they are not one God in three Persons, but three separate Gods),[75] focus on the biblical evidence as well as the patristic (i.e., early Church Fathers) testimony to the Trinity.

Next, point out that the Catholic Church did not originally or immediately have the precise theological nomenclature we have become accustomed to two thousand years hence. Technical theological terminology such as "hypostasis," "*homoousios*" (ὁμοούσιος), and "Trinity" (Latin: *Trinitas,*[76] Greek: Τριάς[77]) only gradually developed in the Catholic Church as her understanding of the divine truths revealed by Jesus and the Holy Spirit deepened.

The Catholic Church did not "invent" new doctrines as it went along but, rather, was able to infer certain truths that are implicit in other, explicit truths. For example, the Old and New Testaments explicitly teach that there is only One God, and yet the Father, Son, and Holy Spirit are each identified explicitly and unambiguously as God (see below for a sketch of this biblical doctrine). When, in A.D. 325, the First Council of Nicaea declared and defined the doctrine of the Trinity, it was able to express the truth of its teaching in clear, unambiguous language that was the fortunate result of three centuries of deep theological reflection and guidance of the Holy Spirit.[78]

A brief sketch of the biblical case for the Trinity can be summarized like this:

> *There is only one God* (Deuteronomy 6:4; Mark 12:29; 1 Timothy 2:5).

> *The Father is God* (Deuteronomy 32:6; Colossians 1:2; Matthew 25:34; Luke 11:2; 1 Corinthians 15:24; Ephesians 4:6; 1 Thessalonians 1:1; John 20:17; Romans 1:7).

> *The Son is God* (Mark 14:61–62; John 1:1–14; 8:58; 20:28; Acts 20:28; 1 Corinthians 10:4; Titus 2:13; Colossians 1:16–17; Philippians 2:5–8; Hebrews 1:8; 1 Peter 5:4; Revelation 1:7, 2:8).

> *The Holy Spirit is God* (John 14:16–17, 26; 16:7–14; Acts 5:3–4; 13:2–4; 21:10–11).

Thus, assuming it is an apologetics discussion with someone who accepts the Bible as inspired and authoritative, we frame the argument that, because the Bible is clear that there is only one God, and because the Father, Son, and Holy Spirit are each declared to be God, then the doctrine of the Trinity — that there is only one God in three Persons — must also be true. This is a deductive argument based on the evidence drawn from Scripture predicated on the *a priori* assumption that the Bible is inspired and authoritative. The Catholic Church chose the Greek term "consubstantiality" to describe the relationship between the three Persons of the Trinity. Another important theological term in explaining the Trinity is *perichóresis* (περιχώρησις), also known as *circumincession*, which refers to the mutual indwelling and consubstantiality of the Three Persons of the Godhead.

Finally, to be well prepared to explain the Blessed Trinity to those who question or disagree with this truth, I strongly recommend you read Frank Sheed's luminous explanation of this truth in *Theology for Beginners* and *Theology and Sanity* (pp. 47–123).

CHAPTER 8

Catholic Apologetics
Making the Case for the Catholic Church

Now let's focus on the structure and internal logic of *Catholic* apologetics, as distinct from natural and Christian apologetics.[79] There is no need to recapitulate here the biblical and historical evidence pertaining to Catholic doctrines — the books I'll recommend later contain that information in abundance. Rather, at the macrolevel, this chapter will consider generally the *process* of making a cogent, persuasive, evidential case for the Catholicity of Christianity.

Whereas all three branches of apologetics (natural, Christian, Catholic) rely on rational proofs, each also requires certain tools uniquely suited to achieving its particular goals. Natural apologetics (demonstrating the existence and nature of God) relies primarily on reason, natural law, and cosmology. Christian apologetics (proving the historicity, divinity, and Resurrection of Jesus) focuses mainly on historical evidence, Old Testament prophecies, and the person, teachings, and miracles of Jesus.

Catholic apologetics deals with those doctrines and practices of the Church Jesus established that are not "mere Christianity" in a generic sense but that are peculiarly and specifically *Catholic*. Generically Christian beliefs include the Trinity and Incarnation. Specifically Catholic doctrines include the Real Presence of Christ in the Eucharist, purgatory, Marian dogmas, and practices such as infant baptism and the Rosary. Keep in mind that in *Catholic* apologetics you are dealing with baptized Christians for whom it's a given that Jesus Christ is true God and true man and the Bible is inspired and trustworthy. So it's not enough to simply quote Bible passages. You must show that the authentic *meaning* of those passages is what the Catholic Church has faithfully taught since the time of Christ and the Apostles. This is why doing Catholic apologetics effectively requires at least a basic command of the pertinent biblical and historical evidence presented in a clear, logical fashion.

There are different permutations of Catholic apologetics, each requiring a particular approach. For example, since Evangelical and Fundamentalist Protestants focus mainly on the Bible, it is the common ground upon which we can build bridges of understanding. Because for them the authority of the Bible takes priority over all else, the case for the Catholic Church must be presented in a thoroughly scriptural way to be effective.

To be sure, you will also need at least a basic command of the facts of Christian history, necessary to strengthen your biblical arguments, especially by demonstrating that the early and medieval Christians were Catholic in every sense of the word.

Apologetics with Evangelical and Fundamentalist Protestants requires the powerful combination of Scripture *and* history. Either one without the other is typically insufficient to do the job properly. For example, it is well and good to demonstrate the truth of the Real Presence of Jesus in the Eucharist with a thoroughgoing appeal to the wide and deep New Testament evidence for this doctrine; but your efforts may well be met with the standard "that's just your interpretation" rejoinder or, worse yet, the "you're just taking that passage out of context" reply. You can defeat that kind of evasive non-answer by employing the historical argument to demonstrate that it's not merely *your* opinion but one that was shared by the early Christians too. A key question to ask in such situations is: "How do you explain that the early Christians believed in the very Catholic doctrine that I am sharing with you? And that they did not agree with what you are suggesting as an alternative understanding of this passage?" The key here is to show the coherence between how the Catholic Church of today expresses a given doctrine and how it was expressed in the early Church. The goal is to show that this coherence is due to the fact that the early Church *was* the Catholic Church.

Your approach to Eastern Orthodox Christians will be considerably different. In their disputes with the Catholic Church, they tend to rely less on the Bible and more on the details of Christian history. Engaging in apologetics discussions with them on the relatively few doctrinal issues that still divide us (e.g., the *filioque* controversy, papal infallibility, and divorce and remarriage) requires due attention to the biblical foundations of these matters, but more importantly you must emphasize the pertinent *historical details* surrounding these differences.

The facts of history loom large when engaging apologetics with Eastern Orthodox believers, not only because they are powerful links in your chain of evidence, but also because our Eastern Orthodox brethren lean heavily on historical arguments in defense of their positions.[80] In this arena, then, it's important to have an adequate grasp of the historical data associated with whatever given issue arises. But don't worry! No one knows everything about Church history. If you are stumped by a question, admit it and let the other person know you'll dig into it and get back to them with an answer. There is no challenge raised against the Catholic Church by the Eastern Orthodox that has not been answered decisively and convincingly, and you have only to do a bit of research to acquire that information.

There are also those who, while at least nominally Catholic, find themselves estranged from the Catholic Church to which they ardently profess to belong. These include various sedevacantist groups[81] and the Society of St. Pius X.[82] Here too, you will almost certainly need to focus on the historical aspects of the Catholic Church that come into play when responding to their challenges (e.g., that the papacy is vacant, that the New Order of the Mass — *Novus Ordo Missae* — promulgated by Vatican II is "invalid," that the so-called "conciliar Church" has plunged completely into heresy and is therefore illegitimate, that there was an "urgent necessity" for Archbishop Lefebvre to defy the express command of Pope John Paul II and consecrate bishops as his successors, et cetera).

Doing apologetics with these groups requires almost entirely a focus on historical issues and ecclesiastical documents, such as the documents of Vatican II and the decrees and other statements of popes and councils.

On the fringes of contemporary Protestantism are the mainline denominations that are steadily shrinking due to scanty conversions, abysmally low fertility rates, and the fact that they have largely abandoned traditional Christian moral principles (e.g., on marriage) and even some Christian doctrines (e.g., the denial of the Resurrection as a real, historical event). The mainline Protestant denominations are withering and may vanish in the not too distant future. This is why Catholics are more likely to have apologetics encounters with Evangelicals and Fundamentalists, who are currently flourishing.[83] A robust biblical presentation of the Catholic Faith, combined with the powerful testimony of the patristic and medieval Church is crucial. A surprisingly large number of Protestants simply do not know what Christianity "looked like" during its first fifteen centuries — the time between the Apostles and Martin Luther. This general unfamiliarity with the facts of Christian history has contributed to an entrenched suspicion for many toward the Catholic Church, regarding it as a bastardized, counterfeit version of true "biblical Christianity." Many Protestants feel that Catholics are not "true" Christians. To remedy this problem, Catholics should strive to be patient, irenic, and respectful, not returning insults in kind but presenting the facts in a friendly, frank, and calm manner. This helps lower barriers of skepticism and dissipate animosity toward the Catholic Church. Patience is key.[84]

Taken together, the doctrines we'll consider now form a "big picture" mosaic of the Catholic Church comprised of numerous "tiles" of Bible passages, elements of Apostolic Tradition, and a body of historical facts. The goal is to put them all together in a coherent and compelling way. And don't worry about the specifics. My book recommendations later on will provide you with everything you'll need to competently engage in Catholic apologetics.

THE CHURCH

The bull's-eye on the target of *Catholic* apologetics is the fact that the Catholic Church is the One, True Church established by Jesus Christ. Everything else flows from this reality. In fact, none of it can be made sense of if this premise isn't established first.

The Catholic Church is not merely one option among many; the Church is not a "denomination" or a "sect" within

Christianity. The Catholic Church is original Christianity
— the ancient Church of Saints Peter and Paul, Clement of
Rome, Ignatius of Antioch, Polycarp, Irenaeus, Justin Martyr, Clement of Alexandria, Maximus the Confessor, Anthony, Athanasius, Ephrem, John Chrysostom, Cyprian of
Carthage, Jerome, Hillary, Ambrose, Damasus, Augustine,
Gregory the Great, and the Cappadocian Fathers. They all
were Catholics, not in merely a "small c" sense of belonging to the "Church universal," but in the fullest sense of the
words "The Catholic Church."[85]

Marshalling relevant quotations from the Church
Fathers will help you show that they were not "generic
Christians" in some amorphous sense, but were Catholics
who preached, wrote, and taught in defense of the Catholic Church — the same Catholic Church of Popes Pius X,
Pius XII, John Paul II, Benedict XVI, and Francis. The goal
is to use their testimony to demonstrate that the Catholic
Church has existed continually down through the centuries, a two-thousand-year span stretching from Jesus and
the Apostles to the present day.

Keep in mind that this Catholic teaching is neither
"antiecumenical" nor "triumphalistic." And it's certainly not
"pre-Vatican II," as is evidenced by section 14 of the Vatican
II document *Lumen Gentium*, in which the Church reiter-
ates this age-old teaching.[86]

There are difficult, perplexing, exasperating, and
sometimes dark chapters in the Catholic Church's long history. To be an effective apologist of integrity and honesty, it's
important that you not make excuses for (i.e., not *apologize*
for) the terrible things that some Catholics have done over
the centuries, including clergy and even a few popes.[87] In
spite of sinful members and a tumultuous history, you can
show, especially by appealing to the teachings of the early

Church Fathers, that the Catholic Church really has stood the test of time as Jesus promised when he said, "And the gates of Hades will not prevail against it" (Matthew 16:18).

Jesus did not establish "Christianity" in the sense of a loose confederation of like-minded people who happen to agree on "the essentials"; he established a Church (Greek: *ekklesía*, ἐκκλησία) to whose leaders, the Apostles, he granted a share in his own authority to preach and teach in his name. As an example of how to take this approach, here are some important passages to use when making this point:

> "He who hears you hears me, and he who rejects you rejects me, and he who rejects me rejects him who sent me." (Luke 10:16)

> "When the Spirit of truth comes, he will guide you into all the truth." (John 16: 13)

> "All authority in heaven and on earth has been given to me. Go therefore and make disciples of all nations, baptizing them in the name of the Father and of the Son and of the Holy Spirit, teaching them to observe all that I have commanded you; and behold, I am with you always, to the close of the age." (Matthew 28:18–20)

These original Apostles understood from Jesus that, since they themselves would eventually die, they were to pass on their ministry as the Church's first bishops by ordaining other men as bishops who, in their turn, would ordain deacons, presbyters, and other bishops for the governance and protection of the Church.[88] This is called "Apostolic Succession" (see CCC 860–862, 1576).[89]

Point out examples of the early Fathers (most notably Sts. Justin Martyr, Irenaeus, and Jerome, as well as Eusebius of Caesarea) who provided a chronology and the names of the successors of St. Peter as the first bishop of Rome — the premier see and exemplar of the reality of apostolic succession in all the other local churches. St. Irenaeus's testimony is hugely important for the apologist to prove this point:

> The blessed apostles [i.e., Peter and Paul], then, having founded and built up the Church, committed into the hands of Linus the office of the episcopate. Of this Linus, Paul makes mention in the Epistles to Timothy. To him succeeded Anacletus; and after him, in the third place from the apostles, Clement was allotted the bishopric. *This man, as he had seen the blessed apostles, and had been conversant with them, might be said to have the preaching of the apostles still echoing [in his ears], and their traditions before his eyes. Nor was he alone [in this], for there were many still remaining who had received instructions from the apostles....* In this order, and by this succession, the ecclesiastical tradition from the apostles, and the preaching of the truth, have come down to us. And this is most abundant proof that there is one and the same vivifying faith, which has been preserved in the Church from the apostles until now, and handed down in truth.[90]

Emphasize the fact that several of these early bishops of Rome *had known the Apostles personally and had been taught the Faith directly by them.* The importance of this very early corroboration of apostolic succession cannot be underestimated, for here we have additional living links in the chain of apostolic succession who were fortunate enough to know for certain the *meaning* of what Peter, Paul, James, and John had written in their epistles. This is proof positive of the transmission of Apostolic Tradition, handed on authoritatively from one generation of the Church to the next, as it has continued down to our present generation.

Explain also that the Catholic Church is a living organism whose external characteristics develop and change as it matures, though it always remains itself. Jesus' parable of the kingdom of heaven being like a mustard seed helps make this point more clearly. The seed matures into a large, treelike plant, just as the Catholic Church of today is the very same Church described in the book of Acts. Though it now looks outwardly different, it remains the same entity.

THE MASS AND THE EUCHARIST

When discussing the subject of the Real Presence of Christ in the Holy Eucharist, I often propose the following question to my non-Catholic discussion partner: "Do you agree that the Catholic Church is either 100 percent right or 100 percent wrong about the Real Presence? In other words, Jesus couldn't be, say 50 percent really present and 50 percent really absent, or 60 percent to 40 percent, or something like that, right? He's either there or he's not; no middle ground, right?" I've never gotten a "no" to that question.

I then point out that if the Catholic Church were in error about this and Jesus is *not* really, substantially, and sacramentally present in the Eucharist under the appearances of bread and wine, then I want nothing to do with the Catholic Church. I would leave, tell everyone else to leave, and never look back. If it's wrong about this one issue, I wouldn't be able to trust it on anything else. And furthermore, this one issue alone is sufficient to blow the Catholic Church out of the water as a claimant to being truly Christian because if it's wrong, it's teaching people to worship *a piece of bread* as if it were God. Nothing could be more diabolical!

However, if the Catholic Church is *right* about the Eucharist and Jesus Christ really is truly, substantially, and sacramentally present under the appearance of bread and wine, then I point out that not only is that a *huge* reason why I am Catholic, it's also a compelling reason for why everyone else in the whole world should be Catholic as well. In other words, make the case right up front, before deploying any of the pertinent Bible verses and historical evidence, that if you can demonstrate, biblically and historically, that the Catholic Church is right about the Real Presence in the Eucharist, then your discussion partner should be willing to consider becoming Catholic. If you have already explained at the outset that you would leave the Catholic Church if its doctrine of the Eucharist can be shown to be false, so then it's only fair and reasonable to ask the other guy if he would be willing to *become* Catholic (or at least seriously consider it) if the situation is reversed and he sees that it is true.

The Bible is replete with explicit and implicit evidence supporting the Catholic teaching on the Eucharist. Make full use of it. The typological Old Testament passages that show us prefigurements of the Eucharist are very important, as is Malachi's prophecy of the Eucharist (Malachi 1:11). And of course the New Testament passages are essential, including those that allude to the Holy Sacrifice of the Mass, such as Hebrews 13:10, "*We have an altar* from which those who serve the tent [i.e., the Jews] have no right to eat," which points to the altar of the Mass in the early Church.

When you quote the Bread of Life Discourse in John 6, be sure to start with the Lord's words in verse 35: "Jesus said to them, 'I am the bread of life; he who comes to me shall not hunger, and he who believes in me shall never thirst.'" (John 6:35). Point out that everything that follows regarding his flesh and blood being "real food" and "real drink" is based on the preparatory phase of "coming" to him in faith and "believing" his teachings.

Some opponents of this biblical truth may try to subvert its plain meaning by claiming that the *only* thing Jesus is teaching here is that we must come to him and believe in him, purporting that it has nothing to do with the Eucharist itself (in the Catholic sense of the word). This is the fallacy of a "false dichotomy" in which an "either-or" option is offered, but this is not true of this passage. It's a "both-and" teaching that encompasses both human faith and the divine reality of the Eucharist.

Again, when approaching this or other Catholic doctrines and practices, bind together the biblical texts with the evidence from the early Church, which is like making a strong, unbreakable rope that can hold the weight of evidence without snapping (see Ecclesiastes 4:12).

THE PRIESTHOOD

Begin by comparing and contrasting the Old Testament priesthood with that which Christ established for the Church in the New Testament, showing that just as the priesthood instituted by God under the Mosaic Law was temporary and largely symbolic, the Catholic priesthood instituted by Jesus is permanent and efficacious because it is *His* priesthood that is imparted. And show that just as all the People of Israel were priests, and God selected and set apart one particular tribe (Levi) to offer sacrifice and minister to the needs of the rest, so too, in baptism, we are all made priests. And yet Christ sets apart certain men through the sacrament of Holy Orders to minister in a particular way to the rest of the baptized faithful.[91]

There could be no valid Eucharist if there were no validly ordained priests. At the Last Supper, Jesus established the two, inextricably intertwined sacraments of the Eucharist and Holy Orders. Each requires the other. The priest offers sacrifice as Jesus commanded when he said, "Do this in memory of me," though this is not a *different* sacrifice from Christ's. The Holy Sacrifice of the Mass, offered for himself, the people, and the whole Church, is not a *repetition* or a *re-enactment* or merely symbolic of Christ's actions at the Last Supper and his atoning Sacrifice on the Cross — his *once for all* sacrifice for our redemption and salvation. Rather, the Mass is the *re-presentation* in time and space of the Lord's once for all sacrifice.

This is why Hebrews 5:6, 7:1 declares that Jesus is our High Priest, the perfect priest and mediator between God and man (see 1 Timothy 2:5), whose priesthood "will never pass away" (Greek: *aparábatos*, ἀπαράβατος). This does not mean that a share in his priesthood is not conferred on priests by virtue of Holy Orders, it means that (1) Jesus alone is our high priest who intercedes for us in heaven with the Father, and (2) his priesthood is "once for all" and eternal. He is *eternally* offering himself as our priest and spotless victim.

THE SACRAMENTS

The main focus when doing apologetics on the sacraments is to show what they are and what they are not:

1. The sacraments are *not* empty, man-made rituals.

2. The sacraments are *not* mere ordinances commanded by Christ, perhaps, but devoid of any really power or supernatural effect.

3. The sacraments are *not* superstitious "hocus pocus."[92]

The sacraments *are*:

1. God's chosen instruments of material things (water, wine, bread, oil, etc.) with which he conveys grace and blessings. This coincides biblically with His love for matter (see Genesis 1:31, "And God saw everything that he had made, and behold, *it was very good*"). Matter is good, and God delights in using it. The Incarnation of Jesus Christ is the highest and best proof of this: "In the beginning was the Word, and the Word was with God, and the Word was God.... And the Word became flesh and dwelt among us" (John 1:1, 14).

2. The sacraments are outward signs *instituted by Christ* to give grace. They *do* what they symbolize, e.g., washing with water is symbolic of the real inward regeneration of washing the soul experiences in the sacrament of Baptism — "God's patience waited in the days of Noah, during the building of the ark, in which a few, that is, eight persons, were saved through water. *Baptism, which corresponds to this, now saves you*, not as a removal of dirt from the body but as an appeal to God for a clear conscience, through the resurrection of Jesus Christ" (1 Peter 3:20–21).

3. It is the power of Jesus Christ working in the sacraments that enables them to cause these profound spiritual changes in the soul; for example, regarding the sacrament of confession, St. Paul declared: "So we are ambassadors for Christ, *God making his appeal through us.* We beg you on behalf of Christ, be reconciled to God" (2 Corinthians 5:20). Also: "*We were buried therefore with Him by baptism* into death so that as Christ was raised from the dead through the glory of the Father, we too might walk in newness of life" (Romans 6:4).

SCRIPTURE AND TRADITION

Protestants adhere to the principle of Scripture Alone (Latin: *sola Scriptura*), which was popularized at the time of the Reformation (revolt). The important thing to be aware of as you do apologetics on this and related topics is that *the Bible nowhere teaches* this principle. Jesus never taught it, the Apostles never taught it or operated according to its dictates, and the early Church never believed it, taught it, or lived according to it.

Simply put, *sola Scriptura* is a false doctrine, a seriously erroneous understanding of the Bible, and a "tradition of men which nullifies the Word of God" (see Matthew 15:1–12; Mark 7:1–15). *Sola Scriptura* imposes a purely human and subjective restriction on Scripture by insisting that the sole infallible interpreter of the Bible is the Bible itself, which simply causes the Bible to be subjected to the vagaries of human opinion. The Bible becomes a Rubik's Cube with which every man tries to understand its meaning for himself.[93]

Point out that Tradition is one main category and both Scripture and unwritten Traditions are subsets of it, two distinct but intimately related modes of transmitting the same gospel. One particularly helpful passage to demonstrate this point is 1 Corinthians 15:1–3. As you read it, point out the following truths it reveals: (1) there is a body of teaching that "you received"; (2) he "preached" this teaching (Greek: *euangelion*, εὐαγγέλιον); we must "hold it fast," that is, Christians are not to ignore or scorn the oral teaching (see 2 Thessalonians 2:15); (3) he first "received" this teaching from the other Apostles and the Holy Spirit and then "delivered" (Greek: *paradidōmi*, παραδίδωμι) it orally; (4) what he preached orally (unwritten Tradition) is "in accordance with" Scripture and is, in fact, an authoritative interpretation of Scripture.

You want to accomplish two key objectives here: First, demonstrate that the Bible nowhere teaches that it is the sole, formally sufficient rule of faith for Christian doctrine and practice.[94] And second, show that the Bible *does* point to the indispensable importance of Apostolic Tradition and that, without recourse to Tradition (i.e., the true *meaning* of the words of Scripture), the Bible's meaning can and will be distorted and twisted.[95]

THE COMMUNION OF SAINTS

One particularly effective biblical case for the Catholic doctrine of the communion of saints (which entails that we may venerate them and invoke their intercession) follows this four-step explanation. After each point, ask the other person if he agrees. Then proceed to the next point. When you reach the conclusion that the saints in heaven are able to (and do) pray for us, it will be much more difficult for your interlocutor to disagree because you have been consistently biblical and logical to reach that point.

1. The Church is the Body of Christ (Romans 12, 1 Corinthians 12).

2. There is only one body of Christ, not one on earth and another one in heaven (1 Corinthians 12).

3. Death does not separate the members of the body (Romans 8:35–39).

4. Christians are bound by the law of Christ to love and pray for one another (1 Timothy 2:1–5).

Quote 1 Timothy 2:1–5 to demonstrate the Bible's standing command that Christians (whether on earth or in heaven) pray for one another.[96] The fact that we cannot understand, in this life, how the Blessed Virgin Mary and the saints in heaven can "hear all those prayers" is not in the slightest a proof that they cannot. There are countless things we were unable to do as babies or young children that we became able to do when we grew up: math problems, drive a car, balance a checkbook, start a business, get a Ph.D., et cetera. Just so, the saints in heaven are *far* more capable of amazing things because they enjoy the perfection of all good things as far as is humanly possible.

SALVATION AND JUSTIFICATION

The Catholic Church's teaching on justification is grounded firmly on Ephesians 2:8–10: "By grace you have been saved through faith; and this is not your own doing, it is the gift of God, not because of works, lest any man should boast. For we are his workmanship, created in Christ Jesus for good works, which God prepared beforehand, that we should walk in them" (Ephesians 2:8–10). It is God's grace from beginning to end, and this grace is a pure gift, for which we can take no credit. Our faith is, thus, a gift of God's grace, as are any good works we may do in grace. We cannot boast about any of it.

Justification is the condition of having been placed by God's grace into a right relationship with him (i.e., having been made righteous). The Council of Trent defines it as our "translation from that condition in which man is born as the son of the first Adam into the state of grace and adoption among the children of God through the Second Adam, Jesus Christ our Savior."[97]

Initial justification, which we receive at baptism,[98] is the starting point for a lifelong progressive process, initiated by the act of God's grace in the soul that is freely accepted,[99] that is continually effected by the infusion of sanctifying grace (primarily through prayer and the sacraments), which is "God's love [that] has been poured into our hearts through the Holy Spirit which has been given to us." We become "new creations" by our justification (see 2 Corinthians 5:17).

Justification and sanctification[100] are two aspects of the same inward reality that God causes in the soul by making us holy through the "renewal of the interior man through the voluntary reception of the grace and gifts, whereby an unjust man becomes a just man, and from being an enemy becomes a friend, that he may be 'heirs in hope of eternal life' (Titus 3:7)."[101]

Sanctification and justification are not two separate things but two sides of the same act of God's grace in us. And good works performed in, by, and through God's in-

dwelling grace are, as St. Paul described them, "the obedience of faith" (Romans 1:5, 16:26) and "faith working
through love" (Galatians 5:6). It is how we cooperate with
God's gift of grace (James 2:22). The process of justifica-
tion/salvation of the Christian, which began with his redemption by Christ, will eventually culminate in salvation and glorification when, after death and the personal
judgment (see Hebrews 9:27), his soul enters heaven and
is counted among the blessed elect who will see God face
to face for all eternity.

Biblical justification is *not*, as Protestants typically
claim, an "extrinsic," "forensic" act of God's grace in which
the "alien righteousness" of Christ is imputed to our souls.
Rather, justification is a real, inward, *intrinsic* change that
God works in our souls by his grace. Justification is not,
as many Protestants claim, a kind of legal fiction in which
God merely imputes the grace of Christ to the soul of the
one justified. While it is true that God does impute Christ's
righteousness to us,[102] his saving grace does far more. It actually accomplishes our regeneration and increase in holiness thereby.

When presenting your case for this Catholic teaching, point out that neither salvation nor justification is a
"one-moment-in-time" event. We rightly say we *have been*
saved (Ephesians 2:8, 2 Timothy 1:9, Titus 3:5), that we *are
being* saved (1 Peter 1:8–9), and that, when we enter into
heavenly glory, we *will be* saved (Romans 5:9–10, 13:11; 1
Corinthians 3:15, 5:5; Philippians 2:12).

The Protestant claims of "eternal security," or an absolute assurance of salvation that can never be lost, must
also be dispelled by the twofold approach of quoting the
Bible verses that make it clear that Christians *can* lose their
salvation followed by an appeal to the patristic testimony

on this point. The Protestant concept of being "once saved, always saved" also entails the notion that when someone is "born again,"[103] he or she is saved by "faith alone," meaning that good works done in grace play no role whatsoever. To explain why this is not biblically true and doesn't conform to the doctrine of the Apostles, show the many verses which speak about the role of good works done in grace.

THE PAPACY

Making the case for the papacy encompasses two primary, interlocking Catholic doctrines: apostolic succession (which we have already discussed) and papal infallibility. The latter entails the fact that the pope, as bishop of Rome and successor to St. Peter, has a special charism of grace, by virtue of his office, promised by Jesus, which prevents him from teaching error to the Church in an official, formal capacity.[104]

A helpful analogy I've relied on to explain this doctrine is that of a steel guard rail around the outer edge of a twisty mountain road where there are steep drop-offs. The rail is analogous to the charism of infallibility in that it prevents the car (the pope) from driving over the edge of the cliff (formally teaching error) during bad weather or if the driver were to fall asleep at the wheel.

Infallibility does not mean that God grants the pope "special knowledge" or inspiration. It does not mean that the pope will always be right in his private opinions about everything, or even anything. Nor does it mean that the pope will be virtuous. Some popes — relatively few — have been corrupt and wicked, and all popes are sinners in need of God's mercy and grace. You must show that papal infallibility protects the Church *from* the pope if the pope were to try to teach error.[105]

You must make the case for both the primacy of Peter among the Apostles as well as the bishops of Rome being his successors. Here again, these issues are inextricable when making the case for Catholic teachings on the papacy. Use the resources in the reading list to demonstrate that Peter had a unique and prominent leadership role among the twelve Apostles. Point out that he is the Apostle most often mentioned by name in the New Testament — some 195 times (e.g., as Peter, Kephas, Cephas, Simon, etc.). By the way, the second most-often mentioned Apostle was St. John (29 times). Whenever all twelve Apostles are listed by name, Peter is always first and Judas is always listed last (Matthew 10:2-5, Mark 3:16-19, Luke 6:14-17, Acts 1:13). Simon is the only Apostle to receive a name change: Simon to Peter (*Kepha*, the Aramaic word for "rock," later translated into Greek as *Petros*[106]). Name changes are rare but hugely significant (e.g., Abram to Abraham, Jacob to Israel). Peter is repeatedly singled out by Jesus for special duties and honors in passages such as Matthew 16:18-19, Luke 22:31-32, John 21:15-17 (see also Acts 1:13-26, 2:14, and Acts chapters 3, 4, 5, 10, 11, and 15).

Using the historical evidence at your fingertips, show also that the early Church recognized the bishop of Rome as having a special primacy of jurisdiction among his brother bishops — something distinct from though related to his status as *primus inter pares* (first among equals). Do this by quoting the many examples of early popes — starting with St. Clement of Rome, in the late first century, *when at least some of the Apostles were still alive* — who taught the Church with a singular kind of authority. Show also the innumerable quotations from the early Church Fathers who appealed continuously to the authority of the pope to settle doctrinal disputes definitively.

The "big picture" goal here is to demonstrate that the vast preponderance of the historical record, as well as the clear and unambiguous biblical evidence surrounding St. Peter, show that he (and by extension, his successors) had been granted by Jesus a unique role as leader of the twelve Apostles.

THE BLESSED VIRGIN MARY

I once described the "Mary problem" many Protestants have this way:

> Mary is much like the stained-glass windows in a beautiful old cathedral: When viewed from the inside, with sunlight streaming through them, the windows are bright and beautiful, explosions of color that are full of meaning. But when viewed from the outside, these same windows can appear dark and drab, devoid of color, and unintelligible. The role of Mary in the Catholic Church can seem just like those windows when viewed from the wrong direction. For many, the Catholic emphasis on her seems superfluous, irrelevant, and even downright objectionable because it all seems to detract somehow from the love and honor we owe to God.[107]

The key Marian doctrines you will need to explain and defend are: Mary's Immaculate Conception (i.e., she was conceived free from original sin and remained free from all actual sin henceforth), her perpetual virginity (i.e., that she neither conceived nor bore any other children aside from Jesus, the biblical mentions of the "brothers of the Lord" notwithstanding), her bodily Assumption (i.e., that, at the end of her earthly life, God translated her time into eternity, body and soul, assuming her into heaven, not permitting her body to molder in the grave.

The case for Mary's Immaculate Conception is more easily made using (especially) typological evidence to show her as fulfillment of the Old Testament types or prefigurements, such as the immaculate cosmos created by God (Genesis 1 and 2); Eve, the natural mother of all humanity, whom God created immaculate and untainted by sin; and the Ark of the Covenant, which contained within itself the Word of God in Scripture (i.e., the Ten Commandments) as well as some pieces of the miraculous manna with which God fed the Israelites while they wandered in the desert for forty years.

Don't be concerned if someone demands that you "prove" the Immaculate Conception or any other Marian doctrine from the Bible. As we've seen, the Bible nowhere claims that it is formally sufficient for doctrine, meaning that more is required to fully elucidate many of the implicit truths it contains by means of Apostolic Tradition. The Bible nowhere states that any given doctrine must be proved from the Bible alone. And the implicit evidence for the Immaculate Conception, taken in concert with the Apostolic Tradition that testifies to this biblical truth, is sufficient to make your case. Note also that even Martin Luther, after he had abandoned the Catholic Church, continued to maintain his belief that Mary was sinless.

With regard to Mary's perpetual virginity, point out that the Bible is actually silent in any explicit fashion on whether or not she had other children besides Jesus. It neither explicitly says she did or that she didn't. But the implicit evidence pointing inexorably to the fact that she remained a virgin, before, during, and forever after the birth of Jesus, is overwhelming and compelling, as you will see in the books I recommend on this topic in the Recommended Resources section.

Similarly, the case to be made for Mary's bodily assumption is not based on any explicit statements to that effect in the Bible. The concept of a bodily assumption is clearly biblical, as is seen in passages such as 2 Kings 2:11 and 1 Thessalonians 4:13–17. Once you have laid out these various biblical evidences, bring in the case from Apostolic Tradition and point out that the testimony of the Church, down through the centuries (see the resources I recommend below for the specific quotes), verifies that though the Bible doesn't speak about Mary's bodily Assumption, it is sufficiently well attested to as to be beyond doubt.

PURGATORY

This doctrine really requires less effort to establish than some other Catholic doctrines. It is eminently biblical (Matthew 18:32–35, 1 Corinthians 3:10–15),[108] and the writings of the early Church Fathers are replete with clear and forceful statements affirming this doctrine. The key to making the case for purgatory is to show first that sin has two distinct but related effects: (1) the eternal punishment and (2) the temporal effects. The eternal punishment for sin can only be expiated and forgiven by God through Jesus Christ's atoning passion and death.

As 1 Timothy 2:5 says, "There is one mediator between God and man, the man Christ Jesus." As our unique mediator, Jesus alone can save us from the eternal penalty due to us for our sins. And purgatory has nothing to do, ultimately, with one's salvation or damnation. Point out that purgatory is *not* a place (condition, state of being) for those who are "too good for hell" but "not good enough for heaven." Nor is purgatory a place where one "gets a second chance" or does anything to "earn" admittance to heaven. Rather, as St. Paul explains in 1 Corinthians 3, it is the way in which God purifies the soul who has built his life "on the foundation" of Jesus Christ and is destined for heaven. The "wood, hay, and straw" of his life's works — that is, all that is incompatible with an all-holy God — must be burned up and purged away before the soul can enter into the glory of heaven (final salvation).

One way to demonstrate this is by asking if the other person is perfect, spotless, and free from sin. Most everyone I've asked this question of says, no, he or she is not perfectly sinless. In that case, you point out, because the Bible says that "nothing unclean" will enter heaven (Revelation 21:27), the same kind of purification must occur between the end of this earthly life and the start of eternity in heaven with God. That process is what the Catholic Church calls purgatory, and it's for this reason that we pray for the souls of the faithful departed.

MORAL ISSUES

Making the case for Catholic moral teachings on subjects like abortion, contraception, traditional marriage (i.e., between one man and one woman), and aspects of human sexuality that pertain to chastity (e.g., fornication, adultery, masturbation, pornography, homosexual activity, etc.) requires a clear and cogent explanation of natural law. Show how even nature reveals to us that things are made for purposes. They have goals and are designed to move toward those goals.

The technical term for the study of this reality is *teleology*. When we misuse a thing in a manner that is contrary to its goal/end, we will ultimately destroy that thing. For example, iPhones are not made for the goal of hammering nails into a wall. Use your iPhone that way and you'll very quickly destroy it. The eye has as its intrinsic, goal-oriented purpose seeing. The ear is ordered toward hearing, and so on. In the same way, the human body's reproductive system is ordered toward procreation. Each of us has a complete nervous system, a complete digestive system, and a complete circulatory system. But none of us has a complete *reproductive system*. Men have one half, and women have the other half. This is one way that natural law sheds light on how we are made by God in such a way that we are apt and capable of fulfilling certain lofty goals, such as procreation — the cooperation with God in His plan of bringing new souls into existence.

In addition to natural law, you must also make your case for Catholic moral teaching by appealing to our common, innate perception that certain things, such as lying, cheating, and stealing, are wrong. These are more obvious than, say, why using artificial contraception is wrong, but pointing them out can be helpful in showing that we have a God-given conscience that helps us recognize — even if only at the level of intuition — that something is wrong with a given activity, warning us to avoid it. The final aspect of this issue centers on the biblical case for Jesus granting the Church, beginning with the Apostles, the authority to teach in His name and with His authority.

CHAPTER 9

You Can't Give What You Don't Have

How to Prepare for Apologetics

Consider this admonition from St. Paul: *"Do your best to present yourself to God as one approved, a workman who has no need to be ashamed, rightly handling the word of truth"* (2 Timothy 2:5). Take this message to heart and put it into practice whenever you engage in apologetics. The Greek word which translates into English as "do your best" is *spoudazō* (σπουδάζω), also rendered as "be diligent." This is a command, not a suggestion!

It's not enough to merely strive to be skillful at apologetics, as if your goals were to "win" arguments and "defeat" the other guy. This mentality is a common "occupational hazard" among those who dabble in apologetics and can even ensnare those who may do apologetics for a living.[109] Those are not the goals of an apologist who wants to rightly handle the word of truth. Rather, your goals are: to be as clear, correct, and compelling as possible in explaining the truths of the Faith. You must aim to be unswervingly charitable, patient, and respectful in the way you defend the truth.

Never lose sight of the fact that your purpose is to help others, to help them see more clearly, and, when the time comes (according to God's timing, not yours), embrace it. For in doing that they are drawing closer to the Lord and thus taking another step toward perfect union with him and an eternity of happiness in heaven. *That* is the goal of apologetics. To help others get to heaven. Everything else, every other motive, is just fluff or frippery.

We're all capable of letting our egos get the better of us, which is probably why the great apologist St. Augustine observed: "He is better advised who acknowledges that even the love of praise is sinful."[110]

Beware also of complacency, the "no problem, I've got this" cavalier attitude toward studying and staying sharp and on your game. It's another subtle pitfall, especially for those who do well naturally and without much effort. That results in its own kind of mediocrity. It might look good on the surface to a casual observer, but is really just a form of coasting. To do apologetics well requires study and, as the Bible says, *diligence*. It's not enough to just "get by" with a superficial understanding of the deep truths you'll be discussing with others.

When St. Paul speaks about "rightly dividing the word of truth," he doesn't mean simply "quoting the Bible." There's much more to the word of truth than just the words on the page. Natural revelation, the Church's liturgy, Apostolic Tradition, the facts of Catholic history, logic, and the vast array of defenses of the Faith that have come from those who came before us are all part of the panoply of truth you must do your best to "rightly divide." It requires some serious, dedicated study, even if that study isn't full-time or conducted within an academic setting.

One good rule of thumb for a novice or an experienced apologist is to get in the good habit of prayerfully reading Scripture each day, even if all you can spend is five minutes. It will not only enhance your spiritual life and relationship with the Lord, it will also expand and deepen your knowledge. Reading Scripture makes you more competent and *confident* when you get into apologetics encounters. And it will serve as a good hedge against complacency and intellectual laziness.

The great Dominican philosopher and spiritual theologian Antonin-Gilbert Sertillanges, O.P. (1863–1948), wrote:

> The great enemy of our knowledge is indolence; that native sloth which shrinks from effort, which does indeed consent now and then capriciously, to make a big effort [i.e., to study] but soon relapses into careless automatism, regarding a vigorous and sustained impetus [i.e., to study] as a regular martyrdom. A martyrdom, perhaps, given our make-up; but we must either be prepared for it or relinquish the idea of study: for what can be done without virile energy? "O God, thou sellest all good things to men at the price of effort," wrote Leonardo da Vinci in his notes. He himself remembered it.[111]

St. Augustine warned about this as well: "Self-complacency is fraught with danger of one who has to beware of pride." And since we all have to beware of pride, that advice is universally applicable. The Bible has a reminder of its own about this: "If it had not been the LORD who was on our side, when men rose up against us, then they would have swallowed us up alive, when their anger was kindled against us" (Psalm 124:2–3).[112]

DO THE RIGHT THING

A firm commitment to honesty and integrity must permeate every aspect of your apologetics efforts. This ranges from accurately and not tendentiously[113] quoting sources to confronting relevant historical data that might be inconvenient to your case.

Following are some "musts" for every apologist:

1. Don't quote selectively in order to make the text appear to say something it really doesn't, which is a form of deception.

2. Handle challenges and opposing arguments fairly, without resorting to straw-man or *ad hominem* fallacies in an effort to dodge their force.

3. Avoid even the hint of plagiarism, especially in what you write.[114]

4. Be willing to admit, when the occasion arises, that an opposing argument makes a good point.

Don't be afraid to admit when you don't know the answer to a question. The worst thing you can do in apologetics is to "wing it" by giving the appearance that you have an answer when you really don't.[115] Be humble. Don't be afraid to say, "I don't know, but I'll find out." That's honest and shows integrity. Even your opponent will respect you for it. When that happens, don't neglect to go *find* the answer, for your own sake as well as that of the other person. There is *nothing*, no question, no challenge, no "problematic" Bible verse or fact of history that Catholic apologists haven't already responded to, thoroughly and compellingly. It's unlikely that anyone could quote a Bible verse to you that the Catholic Church has never been challenged with before!

Also, and just as important, never give in to the temptation to worry or fret that maybe there *is* no good answer. There is. And the beauty part about doing apologetics in the age of the Internet is that a vast wealth of knowledge, experience, and information is quite literally at your fingertips, just a mouse-click away.

Before you can "go forth and do likewise," there are still a few aspects of doing apologetics to consider. They include: how you prepare yourself mentally, intellectually, and, most importantly, *spiritually* for the task ahead.

STUDY THE FAITH

I have already recommended that you study and pray with the Bible every day. I can tell you from experience that if you want to be competent and "equipped for every good work"[116] as an apologist, you need to study diligently what the Church teaches. A few of the resources I've personally found indispensable in this endeavor are:

Ludwig Ott's *Fundamentals of Catholic Dogma* (TAN Books)

Frank Sheed's *Theology and Sanity* (Ignatius Press)

St. Thomas Aquinas' *Summa Theologiae* and *Summa contra Gentiles*

Matthias Scheeben's *Mysteries of Christianity* (B. Herder)

Phillip Hughes' *A History of the Church* series (Sheed & Ward London)

William A. Jurgens' *Faith of the Early Fathers*

Acquire as many good books as you can afford and study them carefully. Remember that you can access huge amounts of information for free on websites like catholic.com and newadvent.org. The point is to study as much and as well as you can so that you'll have the basics (and beyond) down solidly when the time comes to explain or defend them.

PRACTICE DOING APOLOGETICS

You've heard the old saying, "practice makes perfect." While that's not *absolutely* true when it comes to doing apologetics — because there are always more things to learn and more ways to grow and improve — it's close. Simply put, the more you prepare for apologetics through practice, the better you'll get at it. Just like any other occupation, repetition helps you improve. Here's how it works.

You can practice in a few different ways: First, by yourself, in your own mind, thinking through what you would say if someone raised a certain challenge or question. Imagine the situation and ask yourself how you'd respond. What Bible verse or logical argument would you employ? You can do this as a mental exercise while driving to work in the morning or at the end of the day. If you happen to hear a challenge raised on a non-Catholic religious radio or television show, take that opportunity to think through how you might respond. This kind of preparation is like memorizing the times tables. The more you practice and commit information to memory, the more easily you'll be able to access it when the time comes.

Second, practice *Catholic* apologetics scenarios with fellow Catholics who are also interested in apologetics. You can role play and critique each other's answers. Learn from those fictitious dialogues so that when the real thing comes along you won't get caught flat-footed. Some parishes even have informal apologetics groups who meet periodically to discuss things and share information. Another outlet for practicing apologetics with others is online in forums such as those hosted at catholic.com. Maybe you have friends on Facebook or Twitter with whom you can engage in practice discussions.

Third, when you think you're ready, try some "live fire" exercises in which you learn how to do apologetics by having "real-life" discussions with atheists, Protestants, Mormons, and Jehovah's Witnesses. This is really where you'll hone your skills as an apologist. These encounters are often unpredictable (which is good), and you'll have new and different arguments thrown at you (which is good) that will require you to adapt, improvise, and improve on the fly (which is very good!).

I used to *live* for those opportunities when a group of Jehovah's Witnesses or a pair of Mormon missionaries would ring my front doorbell. It's not that I don't welcome those interactions any more; it's just that my house very likely has a big red "don't go there anymore" X across it on the street maps these missionaries use for prospecting calls. When I was younger, I went out of my way to talk to Mormon missionaries because I wanted to learn from them how Mormons make the case for their beliefs. I wanted to hear the best arguments so I could develop even better responses.

Whenever you get the chance, engage in friendly conversation with atheists, Protestants, or others so that you can practice your arguments and techniques. If you saw the 1986 sci-fi thriller movie *Aliens*, you'll understand why. In that movie a brash, young military officer, Lieutenant Gorman, fresh out of the academy and with zero combat or real-life experience, thinks he can defeat the aliens using book learning alone. He quickly finds out how wrong he is.

Flustered and panicky, once he runs out of bluster and answers, he quickly loses control and, because he wasn't prepared for the fight, his life.

Luckily, apologetics isn't nearly so dangerous! Even so, we can learn an important lesson from the hapless, unprepared officer: The more you practice under live conditions, the better apologist you will become. Don't be afraid to get into discussions with atheists. Test out your arguments, including those you learned in this book, for defending your belief in God. You *want* to let those arguments take a beating from the atheist. You *want* to see how well or poorly you constructed your arguments and what he comes back with that you weren't expecting or prepared for. You *want* to experience what it's like to face ridicule and mockery, which comes with the territory, unfortunately, when dealing with some atheists so you will learn better how to keep your cool and not give in to the impulse to lash back and be snarky and mean-spirited in response.

Trust me. One of the most important lessons you'll ever learn in doing apologetics is how to deal with snark. Don't let insults throw you off balance. Even though you will feel angry, don't let a nasty opponent fluster you or make you respond in kind. It's important to learn how to deal with the emotional dimension of apologetics. People naturally tend to get more emotional and less logical when the conversation turns to God and the things of God. This is especially the case if the other guy doesn't believe in God anyway and thinks you're "superstitious" and weak-minded for being a theist.

It's good for you to experience this so that you can learn how to overcome those emotional barriers. As you learned in childhood: Sticks and stones may break my bones, but words will never harm me. True. And it's a snappy way of remembering what Jesus said about persecution: "Blessed are you when men revile you and persecute you and utter all kinds of evil against you falsely on my account. Rejoice and be glad, for your reward is great in heaven, for so men persecuted the prophets who were before you" (Matthew 5:11–12).

Here's how I summarized this elsewhere:

> Bottom line: A cheerful, winsome presentation of the Truth will always do more good for souls than one that is caustic or peremptory, plus it has a far better chance of "getting through" to the other guy. As tempting as it may be to think of yourself as an apologetics gladiator (I have seen many people fall prey to this folly, especially among the current crop of Protestant pop apologists who love nothing more than to "do battle" with Catholics), if you really want to fight the good fight, strive to be polite, respectful, and kind even as you seek to vigorously and compellingly present the truth. Take it from me. As someone who had to learn this lesson firsthand, it really works.[117]

This leads me to another related lesson I learned early on: Be very careful what sources you rely on for "apologetics help," whether books, audio clips, articles, or videos. Not everything that glitters is gold, and not everything that is held out to you as an apologetics "resource" is valuable or trustworthy.

Good example: thirty years ago, when I started getting really into apologetics, I was particularly fascinated by Mormonism. I wanted to learn everything I could about what Mormons believe so that I could understand better how to evangelize them. At that time, there was a very popular book called *The God Makers*, written by Protestant apologists Dave Hunt and Ed Decker. *The God Makers* was quite interesting and even lurid in its "exposition" of key Mormon beliefs. I read it cover to cover. Luckily for me, though, a Mormon I knew told me the book had been answered by some Mormon apologists. I read their articles and was able to see *The God Makers* in a new light, and it wasn't a very flattering one. Hunt and Decker, I discovered, had engaged in shoddy research, tendentious Bible quoting, and fallacious arguments.

As if these serious flaws weren't bad enough, the book is peppered with gratuitous insults against Mormons. Hardly the kind of "honey" to catch flies with. It was instead just a big, slickly written dose of vinegar. In later years, though Ed Decker faded into obscurity, I met Dave Hunt a few times. I saw up-close-and-personal, especially in his anti-Catholic writings and videos, the raw enmity he showed toward the Church. This helped me to see how the old "the enemy of my enemy is my friend" approach is the wrong approach.

When selecting study resources, start first with those that come from unimpeachable Catholic authors and scholars. All the books I've referenced thus far are examples of what I mean. Start with them. Later, when you need to broaden your field of vision, be sure to make use of the books and other resources offered by the group you are dealing with.

If you want to understand atheist challenges, read books by prominent atheists (Dawkins, Hitchens, Harris, Dennett, etc.). It's good to read books and watch videos of debates with atheists. Be sure to get the atheist arguments in their own words so that you can learn how to refute them on their own terms. Ditto for whatever other group or ideology you may be interacting with. Remember too that some Catholics who may have done some important work at one time in the field of apologetics have veered off course theologically or have simply marginalized and even disqualified themselves as trustworthy sources for apologetics information. Be very careful when using, and especially quoting from, their work. Remember that if, in the public mind, so-and-so has a reputation for being a plagiarist, or a shoddy researcher, or "fringy" due to his or her association with controversial groups, movements, or ideologies, you can derail your efforts to do quality apologetics if you are not judicious in how (or if) you cite such sources.

Paradoxically, the converse to this point is also true in a certain sense. A delicate balance in judgment is always necessary.

Bottom line: In all your practice and preparation for apologetics, in all your praying, researching and studying, what you are aiming for is the Truth. As Fr. Sertillanges explains:

> What matters in an idea is not its origin but its magnitude; what is interesting in genius itself is not the person: neither Aristotle, nor Leibnitz, nor Bossuet, nor Pascal, but the truth. The more precious an idea is, the less it matters where it comes from. Train yourself to indifference about sources. Truth alone has a claim, and it has that claim wherever it appears. As we must not swear allegiance to anyone [i.e., to our favorite philosopher, theologian, or apologist], so still less must we disdain anyone; and if it is not expedient to believe everybody, neither must we refuse to believe anyone who can

show his credentials. That is our great liberty. This readiness to accept truth brings so rich a reward.[118]

PRAY, RECEIVE THE SACRAMENTS, AND RELY ON THE POWER OF GOD'S GRACE

We've reached the most important thing of all: the power of God's grace working in and through you. Without this, nothing you do as an apologist will amount to very much. Simply put, in order to effectively share, explain, and defend the Faith, you must really and truly live the Faith. No feigning, no shortcuts, no cheap imitations will do — in other words, don't be a phony. This will do great harm to those around you and to you yourself.

This is the briefest section of this chapter because, although it is the most important, it's also the simplest and most self-evident of all the truths I've endeavored to share with you in this book.

Being a dedicated, committed, all-in, *real* Christian is the only way you will ever amount to anything good and worthy as an apologist. Even if you never do anything related to apologetics, if you never answer someone's challenge or argue in defense of some important truth, if you know and love Jesus, the Father, and the Holy Spirit with all your heart, mind, and strength, then you've done the most important thing of all.

Apologetics is built upon an authentic Christianity, not the other way around. Daily prayer, frequent reception of the sacraments, and an ongoing effort to do good and avoid evil — out of love for God — is the most important part of apologetics. Without that, anything else you might say or do is just so much blather. What's needed most fun-

damentally in the heart of an apologist is love, the supernatural gift of charity. If you want to be a good and effective apologist for truth, meditate often on these words of St.
Paul, one of the greatest apologists ever:

> If I speak in the tongues of men and of angels,
> but have not love, I am a noisy gong or a clang-
> ing cymbal. And if I have prophetic powers,
> and understand all mysteries and all knowl-
> edge, and if I have all faith, so as to remove
> mountains, but have not love, I am nothing. If
> I give away all I have, and if I deliver my body
> to be burned, but have not love, I gain nothing.
> Love is patient and kind; love is not jeal-
> ous or boastful; it is not arrogant or rude. Love
> does not insist on its own way; it is not irritable
> or resentful; it does not rejoice at wrong, but re-
> joices in the right. Love bears all things, believes
> all things, hopes all things, endures all things.
> Love never ends; as for prophecies, they
> will pass away; as for tongues, they will cease;
> as for knowledge, it will pass away. For our
> knowledge is imperfect and our prophecy is
> imperfect; but when the perfect comes, the
> imperfect will pass away. When I was a child,
> I spoke like a child, I thought like a child, I
> reasoned like a child; when I became a man, I
> gave up childish ways. For now we see in a mir-
> ror dimly, but then face to face. Now I know
> in part; then I shall understand fully, even as
> I have been fully understood. So faith, hope,
> love abide, these three; but the greatest of these
> is love. (1 Corinthians 13)

Recommended Resources
Books, Videos, and Audios Arranged by Topic

APOLOGETICS WITH ATHEISTS

The Last Superstition: A Refutation of Modern Atheism, Edward Feser (St. Augustine's Press)

Handbook of Catholic Apologetics, Peter Kreeft and Ronald Tacelli, S.J. (Ignatius Press)

Answering Atheism, Trent Horn (Catholic Answers)

Answering the New Atheism: Dismantling Dawkins' Case against God, Scott Hahn, Benjamin Wiker (Emmaus Road Publishing)

New Proofs for the Existence of God, Robert Spitzer, S.J. (Eerdmans)

Is God a Moral Monster? Making Sense of the Old Testament God, Paul Copan (Baker Books)

God and Evil: The Case for God in a World Filled With Pain, Paul Copan, William Lane Craig, et al. (IVP Books)

Science and the Afterlife Experience: Evidence for the Immortality of Consciousness, Chris Carter (Inner Traditions)

MORAL RELATIVISM

Relativism: Feet Planted Firmly in Mid-Air, Francis Beckwith and Greg Koukl (Baker Books)

Tactics, Greg Koukl (Zondervan)

A Refutation of Moral Relativism: Interviews with an Absolutist, Peter Kreeft (Ignatius Press)

APOLOGETICS WITH PROTESTANTS

Catholicism and Fundamentalism, Karl Keating (Ignatius Press)

Evangelical Is Not Enough, Tom Howard (Ignatius Press)

The Four Witnesses, Rod Bennett (Ignatius Press)

Rome Sweet Home, Scott and Kimberly Hahn (Ignatius Press)

Surprised by Truth, Patrick Madrid (Basilica Press)

Answer Me This!, Patrick Madrid (Our Sunday Visitor)

Envoy for Christ, Patrick Madrid (Servant Books)

On a Mission, Patrick Madrid (Servant Books)

Search and Rescue, Patrick Madrid (Sophia Institute Press)

Why Be Catholic? Ten Answers to a Very Important Question, Patrick Madrid (Doubleday-Image)[119]

APOLOGETICS WITH NON-CHRISTIANS (ISLAM)

Not Peace but a Sword: The Great Chasm between Christianity and Islam, Robert Spencer (Catholic Answers)

GENERAL CATHOLIC APOLOGETICS

Handbook of Catholic Apologetics, Peter Kreeft and Ronald K. Tacelli, S.J. (Ignatius Press)

Fundamentals of the Faith, Peter Kreeft (Ignatius Press)

Orthodoxy, G.K. Chesterton (Ignatius Press)

Radio Replies (three volumes), Leslie Rumble and Charles M. Carty (TAN Books)

Theology and Sanity, Frank J. Sheed (Ignatius Press)

Why Be Catholic? Ten Answers to a Very Important Question, Patrick Madrid (Doubleday-Image)

Envoy for Christ: 25 Years as a Catholic Apologist, Patrick Madrid (Servant Books)

On a Mission: Lessons from St. Francis de Sales, Patrick Madrid (Servant Books)

Search and Rescue, Patrick Madrid (Sophia Institute Press)

Does the Bible Really Say That?, Patrick Madrid (Servant Books)

Where Is That in the Bible?, Patrick Madrid (Our Sunday Visitor)

Why Is That in Tradition?, Patrick Madrid (Our Sunday Visitor)

Answer Me This!, Patrick Madrid (Our Sunday Visitor)

Reasons for Hope, Jeffrey Mirus et al. (Christendom Press)

Reasons to Believe: How to Understand, Explain, and Defend the Catholic Faith, Scott Hahn (Doubleday-Image)

What Catholics Really Believe, Karl Keating (Ignatius Press)

Catholicism and Fundamentalism, Karl Keating (Ignatius Press)

How Not to Do Apologetics, Mark Brumley (Catholic Answers)

We Stand with Christ: An Essay in Catholic Apologetics, Fr. Joseph C. Fenton (The Bruce Publishing Company — out of print, but used copies can be obtained online)

On Guard: Defending Your Faith with Reason and Precision, William Lane Craig (David C. Cook)

How to Defend the Faith without Raising Your Voice, Austin Ivereigh (Our Sunday Visitor)

Defend the Faith!, Robert Haddad (Parousia Media)

Evidence for Our Faith, Fr. Joseph Cavanaugh (Catholic Answers)

Dangers to the Faith, Al Kresta (Our Sunday Visitor)

Catholic Evidence Training Outlines, Frank Sheed, Maisie Ward (Catholic Answers)

Fundamentals of Catholic Dogma, Ludwig Ott (TAN Books)

The Sources of Catholic Dogma, Roy J. Deferrari, trans. (Marian House)

A History of Apologetics, Avery Dulles, S.J. (Ignatius Press)

Theology for Beginners, Frank Sheed (Servant)

Theology and Sanity, Frank Sheed (Ignatius Press)

Apologetics and Catholic Doctrine, Archbishop M. Sheehan, revised by Fr. Peter Joseph (Baronius Press)

DVD

Why Be Catholic?, Patrick Madrid (patrickmadrid.com)

Where Is That in the Bible?, Patrick Madrid (patrickmadrid.com)

Meek and Humble of Heart: How to Engage in Apologetics with Respect and Charity, Patrick Madrid (patrickmadrid.com)

Search and Rescue television series, sixteen parts, Patrick Madrid (patrickmadrid.com)

Catholics and the Culture War, Tim Staples (Catholic Answers)

Truth and Consequences, Tim Staples (Catholic Answers)

AUDIO

The Real Story of the Reformation, Steve Weidenkopf (Catholic Answers)

JESUS CHRIST

Jesus Shock, Peter Kreeft (Beacon Publishing)

Fundamentals of the Faith, Peter Kreeft (Ignatius Press)

The Philosophy of Jesus, Peter Kreeft (St. Augustine's Press)

Handbook of Catholic Apologetics, Peter Kreeft and Ronald Tacelli, S.J. (Ignatius Press)

Jesus: What Catholics Believe, Alan Shreck (Servant Books)

THE PRIESTHOOD

Christ: The Ideal of the Priest, Fr. Columba Marmion (Ignatius Press)

Many Are Called: Rediscovering the Glory of the Priesthood, Scott Hahn (Doubleday-Image)

The Courage to Be Catholic, George Weigel (Doubleday-Image)

The Charism of Priestly Celibacy, John Cavadini (Ave Maria Press)

Priest: The Man of God, His Dignity and Duties, St. John Cafasso (Ignatius Press)

The Priest Is Not His Own, Archbishop Fulton J. Sheen (Ignatius Press)

CD

Did Christ Give Us Priests?: The Priesthood Debate, James Akin vs. Anthony Pezzotta (Catholic Answers)

Celibacy and the Priesthood, Patrick Madrid and Fr. Ray Ryland (patrickmadrid.com)

THE EUCHARIST

The Hidden Manna, Fr. James T. O'Connor (Ignatius Press)

The Eucharist for Beginners: Sacrament, Sacrifice, and Communion, Ken Howell (Catholic Answers)

A Biblical Walk through The Mass, Edward Sri (Ascension Press)

The Lamb's Supper, Scott Hahn (Doubleday-Image)

Consuming the Word: The New Testamant and the Eucharist in the Early Church, Scott Hahn (Doubleday-Image)

Lord, Have Mercy, Scott Hahn (Doubleday-Image)

Jesus and the Jewish Roots of the Eucharist, Brant Pitre (Doubleday-Image)

SCRIPTURE

God's Word: Scripture, Tradition, Office, Cardinal Joseph Ratzinger/Pope Benedict XVI) (Ignatius Press)

The Meaning of Tradition, Cardinal Yves Congar, O.P. (Ignatius Press)

Magisterium: Teacher and Guardian of the Faith, Cardinal Avery Dulles, S.J. (Sapientia Press)

An Essay on the Development of Christian Doctrine, Blessed John Henry Newman (University of Notre Dame Press)

Scripture and Tradition in the Church, Patrick Madrid (Sophia Institute Press)

Why Is That In Tradition?, Patrick Madrid (Our Sunday Visitor)

Envoy for Christ: 25 Years as a Catholic Apologist, Patrick Madrid (Servant Books)

Answer Me This!, Patrick Madrid (Our Sunday Visitor)

Scripture Matters: Essays on Reading the Bible from the Heart of the Church, Scott Hahn (Emmaus Road)

By What Authority? An Evangelical Discovers Tradition, Mark Shea (Our Sunday Visitor)

If Protestantism Is True, Devon Rose (Unitatis Books)

Where We Got the Bible: Our Debt to the Catholic Church, Bishop Henry Graham (Catholic Answers)

100 Biblical Arguments against Sola Scriptura, Dave Armstrong (Sophia Institute Press)

AUDIO

Does the Bible Teach Sola Scriptura?, Patrick Madrid vs. James White (debate, patrickmadrid.com)

Search the Scriptures, Patrick Madrid vs. Rowland Ward (debate, patrickmadrid.com)

The Bible-Only Debate, Patrick Madrid and Karl Keating vs. Bill Jackson and Ron Nemec (patrickmadrid.com)

What Still Divides Us?, Patrick Madrid et al. vs. Michael Horton et al. (patrickmadrid.com)

THE COMMUNION OF SAINTS

Angels and Saints: A Biblical Guide to Friendship with God's Holy Ones, Scott Hahn (Doubleday-Image)

Any Friend of God's Is a Friend of Mine: A Biblical and Historical Explanation of the Communion of Saints, Patrick Madrid (Basilica Press)

Why Be Catholic? Ten Answers to a Very Important Question, Patrick Madrid (Doubleday-Image)

AUDIO

The Communion of Saints Debate, Patrick Madrid vs. James White (patrickmadrid.com)

Winning Souls, Not Just Arguments, Patrick Madrid and Curtis Martin (patrickmadrid.com)

SALVATION AND JUSTIFICATION

A Father Who Keeps His Promises, Scott Hahn (Doubleday-Image)

First Comes Love, Scott Hahn (Doubleday-Image)

The Drama of Salvation, Jimmy Akin (Catholic Answers)

Catholicism and Fundamentalism, Karl Keating (Ignatius Press)

Salvation Is from the Jews, Roy H. Schoeman

Predestination: The Meaning of Predestination in Scripture and the Church, Fr. Reginald Garrigou-Lagrange, O.P. (TAN Books)

Life Everlasting, Fr. Reginald Garrigou-Lagrange, O.P. (TAN Books)

AUDIO

What Still Divides Us?, Patrick Madrid et al. vs. Michael Horton et al. (patrickmadrid.com)

THE PAPACY

Upon This Rock, Steve Ray (Ignatius Press)

Pope Fiction: Answers to 30 Myths and Misconceptions about the Papacy, Patrick Madrid (Basilica Press)

The Shepherd and the Rock, Archbishop J. Michael Miller (Our Sunday Visitor)

And on This Rock, Fr. Stanley L. Jaki (Trinity Communications)

The Office of Peter and the Structure of the Church, Fr. Hans Urs von Balthasar (Ignatius Press)

Early Christian Doctrines, J.N.D. Kelly (Harper Collins)

Rome and the Eastern Churches, Fr. Aiden Nichols, O.P. (The Liturgical Press)

The Popes and Slavery, Joel S. Panzer (Alba House)

The Bones of St. Peter, John Evangelist Walsh (Sinag-Tala Press)

Jesus, Peter, and the Keys, David Hess et al. (Queenship)

AUDIO

Why Do We Have a Pope?, Scott Hahn (lighthousecatholic media.com)

Pope Fiction television series (thirteen episodes, patrickmadrid.com)

MARY

Behold Your Mother, Tim Staples (Catholic Answers)

Any Friend of God's Is a Friend of Mine, Patrick Madrid (Basilica Press)

Walking with Mary: A Biblical Journey from Nazareth to the Cross, Edward Sri (Doubleday-Image)

Hail, Holy Queen, Scott Hahn (Doubleday-Image)

The Immaculate Conception of the Mother of God, Bishop William B. Ullathorne (Christian Classics)

Mary through the Centuries, Jaroslav Pelikan (Yale University Press)

Mary: A History of Doctrine and Devotion, Hilda Graef (Christian Classics)

The Thousand Faces of the Virgin Mary, George H. Tavard (Michael Glazier Books)

Mary in the Middle Ages, Fr. Luigi Gambero, S.M. (Ignatius Press)

Mary and the Fathers of the Church, Fr. Luigi Gambero, S.M. (Ignatius Press)

Refuting the Attack on Mary, Fr. Mateo (Catholic Answers)

LOGIC AND ARGUMENTATION

Socratic Logic, Peter Kreeft (St. Augustine's Press)

On a Mission: Lessons from St. Francis de Sales, Patrick Madrid (Servant Books)

Search and Rescue: How to Bring Your Family and Friends into (or Back into) the Catholic Church, Patrick Madrid (Sophia Institute Press)

Why Good Arguments Often Fail, James W. Sire (IVP Books)

The Gentle Art of Verbal Self-Defense, Suzette H. Elgin (Dorset House)

On Guard: Defending Your Faith with Reason and Precision, William Lane Craig (David C. Cook)

In the Line of Fire: How to Handle Tough Questions — When It Counts, Jerry Weissman (Pearson FT Press)

Tactics: A Game Plan for Discussing Your Christian Convictions, Gregory Koukl (Harper Collins)

ATHEISM AND AGNOSTICISM

The Godless Delusion: A Catholic Critique of Modern Atheism, Kenneth Hensley and Patrick Madrid (Our Sunday Visitor)

The Last Superstition: A Refutation of the New Atheism, Edward Feser (St. Augustine's Press)

Philosophy of Mind: A Beginner's Guide, Edward Feser (Oneworld Publications)

Theology and Sanity, Frank Sheed (Ignatius Press)

Answering the New Atheism: Dismantling Dawkins's Case against God, Scott Hahn and Benjamin Wiker (Our Sunday Visitor)

Something Other Than God, Jennifer Fullwiler (Ignatius Press)

Not God's Type: An Atheist Academic Lays Down Her Arms, Holly Ordway (Ignatius Press)

A Concise Introduction to Logic, Patrick J. Hurley (Wadsworth Publishing)

Answering Atheism, Trent Horn (Catholic Answers)

LIFE ISSUES

Persuasive Prolife, Trent Horn (Catholic Answers)

Life Issues, Medical Choices, Janet Smith and Christopher Kaczor (Servant Books)

STUDY THE FAITH

Fundamentals of Catholic Dogma, Ludwig Ott (TAN Books)

Theology and Sanity, Frank Sheed (Ignatius Press)

Summa Theologiae, St. Thomas Aquinas

Summa contra Gentiles, St. Thomas Aquinas

Mysteries of Christianity, Matthias Scheeben (B. Herder)

A History of the Church series, Philip Hughes (three volumes, Sheed & Ward London)

Faith of the Early Fathers, William A. Jurgens (three volumes, Liturgical Press)

Notes

1 Championed by notable figures in history such as the Catholic philosopher Roger Bacon (1214–1294), a Franciscan friar who is widely recognized as having been a significant late-medieval promoter of the empirical method for testing scientific claims, especially as it had been pioneered by Aristotle some 1500 years earlier.

2 "The Case for Life After Death," *Truth: An International, Inter-Disciplinary Journal of Christian Thought*, Volume 1 (1985).

3 For example, "The church of God which sojourns at Rome to the church of God which sojourns at Corinth.... But if any disobey the words spoken by him through us, let them know that they will involve themselves in transgression and in no small danger." (Clement of Rome, Pope, First Epistle to the Corinthians, 1, 59:1)

4 American Airlines' frequent flier program is my friend. Like baseball was for Garrett Morris's SNL character, I can say the 2.5 million miles I've racked up with American over the years have been very, very good to me in terms of free upgrades.

5 Frank Sheed explains what this means and what it does not mean: "There may still remain one error clinging to our knowledge of the processions of the Persons of the Trinity because of our own immersion in time.... [T]here is no succession in eternity, no change in God. God the Father did not first exist as a person and then become a Father. God, by the very act of being God, generates His Son. God the Father and God the Son, by the very act of being God spirate the Holy Spirit.... Because time is so deeply woven into all our experience, our advance in the knowledge of God depends upon our deliberate effort to rid our mind of it. The trouble is that we have no language for what we are trying to say. We cannot make any statement at all without tenses, past or present or future; but God's actions have no tense. He has no past; he has no future. He has only an eternal present, but it is not our present, poised between past and future; it is not a tense at all. How then are we to utter God's actions with man's verbs? Our nearest tense to his timelessness is the present tense" (Frank Sheed, *Theology and Sanity*, pp. 108–109).

6 I name names and give real-life examples of such debate-inspired conversions in my book *Envoy for Christ: 25 Years as a Catholic Apologist* (Cincinnati: Servant Books, 2012). This kind of conversion is much more common than one might imagine.

7 Patrick J. Hurley, *A Concise Introduction to Logic* (Belmont, CA: Wadsworth Publishing Company, 1994), and Peter Kreeft, *Socratic Logic* (South Bend: St. Augustine's Press, 2004, 3rd edition).

8 Peter Kreeft, *Socratic Logic*.

9 Ibid., pp. 1–2, 4. Emphasis in the original.

10 Ibid., p. 32.

11 Ibid., p. 29.

12 John D. McKinnon, "GOP Lawmakers Grill IRS Chief Over Lost Emails," *Wall Street Journal*, June 20, 2014. Available electronically at http://on.wsj.com/1rQTywl.

13 Ian Byrd of www.byrdseed.com.

14 Attributed to the fourth-century Roman Emperor Constantius II, addressed to Pope Liberius, "Why do you support Athanasius against the world?" at the height of the Arian controversy.

15 Hurley, p. 1.

16 Ibid., p. 2.

17 Kreeft, p. 29.

18 Ibid., p. 29.

19 Dictionary.com.

20 The common pronunciation in English is ápophatic.

21 A common rejoinder to this truth claim is, "What about the devil? God created him, and *he* certainly isn't good." The fact that God did indeed create the devil is not a contradiction of the fact that God only creates good things because God created the devil as a good angel. But when he (Lucifer), in his pride, rebelled against God, he became evil.

22 A helpful explanation of how Calvinists use the presuppositional apologetics method is found in Cornelius Van Til's essay "My Credo," printed in *Jerusalem & Athens: Critical Discussions on the Philosophy and Apologetics of Cornelius Van Til* (Presbyterian & Reformed Publishing Co., Phillipsburg, NJ: 1971). Van Til describes the presuppositional approach as an apologetics "focusing on the self-attesting Christ of Scripture … which attempts to understand his world through the observation and logical ordering of facts in self-conscious subjection to the plan of the self-attesting Christ of Scripture." Van Til further explains that in presuppositional apologetics, "we use the same principle in apologetics that we use in theology: the self-attesting, self-explanatory Christ of Scripture…. [W]e no longer make an appeal to 'common notions' which Christian and non-Christian

agree on, but to the 'common ground' which they actually have because man and his world are what Scripture says they are.... [W]e appeal to man as man, God's image. We do so only if we set the non-Christian principle of the rational autonomy of man against the Christian principle of the dependence of man's knowledge on God's knowledge as revealed in the person and by the Spirit of Christ.... [W]e claim, therefore, that Christianity alone is reasonable for men to hold. It is wholly irrational to hold any other position than that of Christianity. Christianity alone does not slay reason on the altar of 'chance,' ... [and] we argue, therefore, by 'presupposition.' The Christian, as did Tertullian, must contest the very principles of his opponent's position. The only 'proof' of the Christian position is that unless its truth is presupposed there is no possibility of 'proving' anything at all. The actual state of affairs as preached by Christianity is the necessary foundation of 'proof' itself."

23   An historical novelty that has its provenance primarily in the apologetics writings of John Calvin and his disciples.

24   For a comprehensive, if excruciatingly long, tedious, and ultimately ineffective, attempt by a Calvinist to discredit evidential apologetics, see Greg Bahnsen, "A Critique of the Evidentialist Apologetical Method of John Warwick Montgomery," cmfnow.com/articles/PA016.htm.

25   Avery Dulles, S.J., *A History of Apologetics* (San Francisco: Ignatius Press, 1999), p. 357.

26   See Patrick Madrid, *Scripture and Tradition in the Church* (Manchester: Sophia Institute Press, 2014).

27   Of course, there are subissues here that we'll deal with later in the book. But for now, I want you to see the broad categories of commonality, even if there are serious differences in other areas.

28   Russian Orthodox, Greek Orthodox, et cetera; and the Eastern Patriarchates of Constantinople, Alexandria, Antioch, and Jerusalem. A very helpful book to better understand the theological and juridical issues that separate the Eastern Orthodox Churches from the Catholic Church is Aiden Nichols, O.P.'s *Rome and the Eastern Churches* (Collegeville, MN: The Liturgical Press, 1992). To better understand Orthodox beliefs and customs, see Daniel B. Clendenin, *Eastern Orthodox Theology* (Grand Rapids: Baker Academic, 1995).

29   For an extremely thorough explanation, based on Scripture and Apostolic Tradition, why the Catholic Church does not permit divorce and remarriage, including a critique of the Eastern Orthodox acceptance of it, see Robert Dodaro, O.S.A., ed., *Remaining in the Truth of Christ: Marriage and Communion in the Catholic Church* (San Francisco: Ignatius Press, 2014).

30 Non-church-going Catholics who have at best a nominal connection to the Church are likely to have a far more rudimentary understanding of Church teaching.

31 The euphemism "to know" someone refers to having carnal knowledge of him or her — that is, to have sexual relations.

32 Jordan Aumann, O.P., *Spiritual Theology* (Collegeville: The Liturgical Press, 1980), p. 140.

33 Sometimes, you may discern that, objectively speaking, the person in question was not in fact wronged, but simply feels aggrieved. That's okay. Whatever the experience was that caused the anger, you can still seek to build a bridge over those troubled waters by acknowledging simply that it happened and that you empathize.

34 Pope St. John Paul II was very attentive to this important though sometimes difficult Christian duty. For example, in 1999, during his pontificate, an extraordinary document called *Memory and Reconciliation: The Church and the Faults of the Past* was promulgated in which the Catholic Church apologized for a variety of things Catholics have done over the centuries to cause injury and suffering to others.

35 Frank Sheed, *Theology for Beginners*, 3rd edition (Ann Arbor: Servant Books, 1981), p. 17. Sheed was one of the greatest and most effective Catholic apologists of the twentieth century. For a sketch of his life and his life's work, see my book *Envoy for Christ: 25 Years as a Catholic Apologist* (Cincinnati: Servant Books, 2012), pp. 149–157.

36 Dictionary.com.

37 Ibid.

38 "I have fought the good fight, I have finished the race" (2 Timothy 4:7; see also 1 Corinthians 9:24–27); the potter (God) and the clay pot (Romans 9:19–23); the cultivated and wild olive trees (Romans 11:17–24).

39 For a humorous yet theologically insightful take on St. Patrick and the Shamrock, watch Lutheran Satire's "St. Patrick's Bad Analogies" video on YouTube.

40 Ninety-nine percent of human language is comprised of natural-order words.

41 Watchtower Bible and Tract Society of Pennsylvania (Brooklyn: International Bible Students Association, 1989).

42 Ibid., pp. 3–4, emphasis added.

43 Dictionary.com.

44 This approach comprises a significant part of Richard Dawkins's efforts to debunk theism in his book *The God Delusion* (New York: Mariner Books, 2006), see pp. 68–77. Scott Hahn and Benjamin Wiker offer a Catholic refutation of his arguments in *Answering the New Atheism: Dismantling Dawkins' Case against God* (Steubenville: Emmaus Road Publishing, 2008).

45 Geoffrey Mohan, "Scientists Seek Religious Experience — in the Brain," sci-tech-today.com, January 7, 2015.

46 Pages 52–94.

47 *The Physics*, book IV.

48 *Handbook of Catholic Apologetics*, p. 54.

49 The Hubble Telescope has contributed an immense amount of scientific data demonstrating that the universe isn't simply in motion, it is expanding rapidly, galaxies speeding away from each other. For an overview of these findings, see Mario Livio, "The Expanding Universe: Lost (in Translation) and Found" (hubblesite.org).

50 The "universe" is defined as "the totality of spacetime and everything that exists therein, including all planets, stars, galaxies, the contents of intergalactic space, the smallest subatomic particles, and all matter and energy" ("Universe," *Webster's New World College Dictionary* [Hoboken, NJ: Wiley Publishing, Inc., 2010]).

51 *Handbook of Catholic Apologetics*, p. 59. Emphasis in the original.

52 See Michael Behe, William Dembski, Stephen Meyer, *Science and Evidence for Design in the Universe* (San Francisco: Ignatius Press, 2003).

53 (Grand Rapids: Wm. B. Eerdmans Publishing Company, 2010).

54 *God, Actually: Why God Probably Exists, Why Jesus Was Probably Divine, and Why the "Rational" Objections to Religion Are Unconvincing* (Oxford: Monarch Books, 2012), p. 46.

55 As distinct from the supernatural virtues that come through God's grace and our cooperation by faith, see Ephesians 2:8–10.

56 Kreeft and Tacelli, *Handbook of Catholic Apologetics*, pp. 129–130.

57 Lactantius, *The Anger of God*, 4.

58 Aquinas, *Summa Theologiae* 1, 2, 3, Obj. 1, summarized by Kreeft and Tacelli in *Handbook of Catholic Apologetics*, p. 128.

59 C.S. Lewis, *The Problem of Pain*, in *The Complete Works of C.S. Lewis Signature Classics* (New York: Harper San Francisco, 2002), p. 379. Every student of apologetics should read *The Problem of Pain* to see and profit from

Lewis's convincing demonstration that this argument *is* eminently answerable. This summary is given in Kreeft and Tacelli, *Handbook of Catholic Apologetics*, p. 128.

60 Robert B. White, *Who Is to Blame? Disasters, Nature, and Acts of God* (Grand Rapids, MN: Monarch Books, 2014), passim.

61 White, p. 157.

62 Named for the seventeenth-century French mathematician and philosopher (1623–1662) who devised this challenge to atheists as a way to encourage them to reconsider the case for God's existence.

63 Joseph Lataste, "Blaise Pascal," *The Catholic Encyclopedia* (New York: Robert Appleton Company, 1911), vol. XI.

64 "Still a Firebrand, 2,000 Years Later: Zealot: 'The Life and Times of Jesus of Nazareth," *New York Times*, August 5, 2013, http://nyti.ms/1ylabQq.

65 Contemporary biblical scholars and historians of the historical era in which Jesus lived overwhelmingly agree that there is no question but that he did live when and where the New Testament says he did. Richard A. Burridge, Dean of Kings College (London) and professor of biblical exegesis, states: "There are those who argue that Jesus is a figment of the Church's imagination, that there never was a Jesus at all. I have to say that I do not know any respectable critical scholar who says that any more" (Richard A. Burridge, Graham Gould, *Jesus Now and Then* [Grand Rapids: William B. Eerdmans Publishing Company, 2004, p. 34]). The late British classicist and historian of antiquity, Michael Grant (1954–2004), wrote: "Modern critical methods fail to support the Christ-myth theory. It has again and again been annihilated by serious scholars. In recent years, 'no serious scholar has ventured to postulate the non-historicity of Jesus' or at any rate very few, and they have not succeeded in disposing of the much stronger, indeed very abundant, evidence to the contrary" (*Jesus: An Historian's Review of the Gospels* [New York: Simon & Schuster, 1992], p. 200).

66 See Acts 9:1–2: "But Saul, still breathing threats and murder against the disciples of the Lord, went to the high priest and asked him for letters to the synagogues in Damascus, so that if he found any belonging to the Way, men or women, he might bring them bound to Jerusalem."

67 Louis H. Feldman, trans., *The Loeb Classical Library*. Take note of the various scholarly comments about this passage, which are summarized on Wikipedia: http://bit.ly/1xuG70S.

68 An interesting side note: The Christian writer Sextus Julius Africanus (A.D. 160–240) refers to the now lost writings of a first-century pagan named Thallus (d. A.D. 52) who ventured an explanation for a period of intense

darkness and a massive earthquake that occurred at the same time that the Gospels say Jesus was crucified. Although Thallus did not (at least according to Africanus) write about Jesus himself, it's worth noting that he does corroborate the fact that some phenomenon of darkness and an earthquake happened in a way that tracks with the biblical account. For details on Africanus's *Cronography,* see: the Christian Classics Ethereal Library http://bit.ly/154Vs1K. Africanus (as well as Origen) also quotes a certain Phlegon, a pagan historian of the mid-second century whose works have been lost but who wrote about Jesus and described the strange darkness that covered the land and the earthquake that struck at the hour of Jesus' death on the cross.

69 *The Annals,* XV, 44; available electronically at http://www.sacred-texts.com/cla/tac/a15040.htm. In this same passage, Tacitus describes the bloody persecution of Christians in Rome, who were made to be scapegoats by Nero in his attempt to deflect blame from himself for the fire. "Accordingly, an arrest was first made of all [Christians] who pleaded guilty; then, upon their information, an immense multitude was convicted, not so much of the crime of firing the city, as of hatred against mankind. Mockery of every sort was added to their deaths. Covered with the skins of beasts, they were torn by dogs and perished, or were nailed to crosses, or were doomed to the flames and burnt, to serve as a nightly illumination, when daylight had expired. Nero offered his gardens for the spectacle, and was exhibiting a show in the circus, while he mingled with the people in the dress of a charioteer or stood aloft on a car. Hence, even for criminals who deserved extreme and exemplary punishment, there arose a feeling of compassion; for it was not, as it seemed, for the public good, but to glut one man's cruelty, that they were being destroyed" (ibid.).

70 http://ancienthistory.about.com/library/bl/bl_text_plinyltrstrajan.htm.

71 Note that death by stoning was a punishment prescribed by the Law of Moses for only a relatively few religious crimes (outlined in the books of Leviticus and Deuteronomy), one of which was to blaspheme the name of God, given to Moses in Exodus 3 (see jewishencyclopedia.com).

72 Such as the Tractate "Sanhedrin" (43a) in the Babylonian Talmud.

73 See Kreeft and Tacelli, *Handbook of Catholic Apologetics,* pp. 186–219, for a detailed and comprehensive explanation of all the major and minor issues at work in making the case for the Resurrection.

74 Ibid., p. 152.

75 The official website of the Mormon Church declares the following: "There are three separate persons in the Godhead: God, the Eternal Father; his Son, Jesus Christ; and the Holy Ghost. We believe in each of them. From latter-

day revelation we learn that the Father and the Son have tangible bodies of flesh and bone and that the Holy Ghost is a personage of spirit, without flesh and bone. These three persons are one in perfect unity and harmony of purpose and doctrine" (lds.org/scriptures/gs/god-godhead).

76 Tertullian (died c. 180) uses the Latin *trinitas* in an explanation of the Trinity in *On Modesty*.

77 Theophilus of Antioch coined the term "Trinity" (Τριάς) in his Epistle to Autolycus (A.D. 180).

78 Elsewhere, I explain this development of doctrine this way: "From these explicit truths, and under the guidance of the Holy Spirit, who guides the Church 'into all truth' (John 16:12–13; see 14:25–26), the Catholic Church teaches that if there is only one God, and if the Father, Son, and Holy Spirit are each God, then the doctrine of the Trinity — one God in three Persons — must also be true. Otherwise, these revelations become a jumbled mass of irreconcilable contradictions. And though one will not find the word 'Trinity' in Scripture, the above passages point us toward the doctrine, which God revealed gradually, indirectly and in various ways (Hebrews 10:1)....

"Old Testament episodes known as theophanies — mysterious appearances of one or more Persons of the Trinity ... are found in Genesis 1:26 (where God speaks of himself in the plural form); 3:22; 11:27; 18; Psalm 2:7; 109:1–3; Isaiah 7:14 (Immanuel means "God with us"); 9:6; 11:2 and 35:4.... Proverbs 8:22–31; Wisdom of Solomon 7:22–28; 8:3–8; Ezekiel 11:5, 36:27; Joel 2:28 and Malachi 3:1.... [See also] Matthew 28:18–19 and John 1:1, 14...." (Patrick Madrid, *Does the Bible Really Say That?* [Cincinnati: Servant Books, 2006], pp. 59–60).

79 Catholic apologetics (as distinct from natural and Christian apologetics) has had a certain priority among Western Catholics, aimed at responding to challenges raised by Protestants, even as a return to natural and Christian apologetics becomes increasingly important, given the rapid rise of militant atheism and aggressive forms of secularism, as well as challenges posed by Islam, Mormonism, Jehovah's Witnesses, and other groups whose doctrines contradict and even attack fundamental Christian truths.

80 The late Fr. Ray Ryland wrote many very insightful apologetics articles on Catholic-Orthodox issues, and I encourage every aspiring Catholic apologist to read and make use of his cogent arguments and emulate his irenic style.

81 That is, those who argue that the office of papacy is currently vacant and the chair (*sēdēs*) of Peter is vacant (*vacāns*), this due to the alleged heresy or malfeasance of a pope, or the lack of a validly conducted papal conclave.

82 Some Catholic apologetics issues pertain to those who are in the Catholic Church yet are in some way in doctrinal or praxis-related conflict with the Church, some even claiming that *they* represent the Church and that everyone else is in conflict with *them*. Sedevacantist groups and certain radical traditionalist groups fall into this category. In certain respects, though members of these groups consider themselves staunch Catholics, *real* Catholics, they find themselves in ongoing strife and struggle with the very Church to which they profess their allegiance.

83 Beginning in earnest in the late nineteenth century and carrying forward into the early twentieth, a great struggle arose within Protestantism in England and the United States over the gradual but relentless trend in Protestant seminaries toward abandoning key beliefs of Christianity (e.g., the Virgin birth; the Resurrection as a real, literal, historical event; the miracles of Jesus, etc.) in favor of a "demystified" understanding of Jesus and his teachings. In the Catholic Church this has been known as the heresy of Modernism (see Pope St. Pius X's 1907 encyclical *Lamentabili Sane*).

84 See my discussion of this issue of Protestantism's "anti-Roman complex" in *Scripture and Tradition in the Church* (Manchester: Sophia Institute Press, 2014), pp. 43–64.

85 The historical identity of the Catholic Church and its claim that it has perdured for two thousand years *incudes* those Churches which we know today as the Eastern Orthodox Churches. The Eastern Churches were all part of the One, Holy, Catholic, and Apostolic Church until the eleventh century when, tragically, they broke communion with the Bishop of Rome and thenceforth have lived apart from the Catholic Church, though with valid holy orders and sacraments. They, too, trace themselves back to Christ and the Apostles through the Catholic Church.

86 "This Sacred Council wishes to turn its attention firstly to the Catholic faithful. Basing itself upon Sacred Scripture and Tradition, it teaches that the Church, now sojourning on earth as an exile, is necessary for salvation. Christ, present to us in His Body, which is the Church, is the one Mediator and the unique way of salvation. In explicit terms He Himself affirmed the necessity of faith and baptism and thereby affirmed also the necessity of the Church, for through baptism as through a door men enter the Church. Whosoever, therefore, knowing that the Catholic Church was made necessary by Christ, would refuse to enter or to remain in it, could not be saved" (see also section 8).

87 Especially clergy and popes. Lay Catholics have certainly contributed their share of scandal over the centuries, but the real headline-grabbing moral failures have typically been those of the clergy, at least in the sense that

they are more sensational because priests and bishops are understood to be held to a higher standard of Christian rectitude, and when they fail to live up to that standard and cause scandal, it's magnified in the minds of onlookers, especially non-Catholics.

88 "The power to ordain belongs to those who are consecrated bishops, thus receiving the fullness of the sacrament of holy orders" (Patrick Madrid, *Why Be Catholic? Ten Answers to a Very Important Question* [New York: Doubleday-Image, 2014], p. 213). See also CCC 1554.

89 To make a compelling biblical case for Apostolic Succession, I recommend deploying passages in this sequence: Acts 1:15–26; 1 Thessalonians 2:6–7; 2 Timothy 1:6; Acts 14:23, 20:28; 1 Corinthians 12:27–29; Ephesians 4:11, 2:20; 1 Thessalonians 1:1–2:12; 1 Timothy 3:1–8, 4:13–14, 5:17–22; 2 Timothy 2:1–2; Titus 1:5–9.

90 *Against Heresies*, 3:3:3.

91 For a comprehensive explication of this dimension of the Catholic priesthood, see the "Did Christ Give Us Priests?" public debate between Jimmy Akin (Catholic) and Anthony Pezzotta (Protestant). See also Tim Staples, "The Priesthood Is Both Ministerial and Universal" (*This Rock* magazine, March 2010, vol. 21, no. 2).

92 A common source for this notion is the Chick tract "The Death Cookie," a Fundamentalist comic book that derides the Holy Eucharist claiming it is really a pagan holdover in the Catholic Church. I described it: "The tract then depicts these 'Holy Helpers,' who are dressed as Catholic monks, intoning 'hocus pocus domi nocus' over a cookie/host with the fingers of both hands extended toward it as if arcs of electricity would flow from them. A bit of faux Latin doggerel intended to mock the Latin words of consecration at the Mass, where the priest says, '*Hoc est enim corpus meum*' ('This is my body')." (Patrick Madrid, *Why Be Catholic?*, pp. 65–66, 214.)

93 The Calvinist Westminster Confession of Faith makes this fatal defect in *sola Scriptura* blindingly clear. Available electronically at http://www .reformed.org/documents/wcf_with_proofs.

94 For several examples of this in debate format, see my public debates with Protestant ministers on this subject. See especially my debate with James White "Does the Bible Teach *Sola Scriptura*?" and "What Still Divides Us?" — available in CD format or as digital downloads at patrickmadrid.com/ store/debates.

95 For a detailed explanation of both points, see Patrick Madrid, *Scripture and Tradition in the Church* (Manchester: Sophia Institute Press, 2014);

Why Is That in Tradition? (Huntington, IN: Our Sunday Visitor, 2002); *Envoy for Christ* (Cincinnati: Servant Books, 2012, pp. 4–52).

96 See my book *Now What? A Guide to the Catholic Church for New (and Not-So-New) Catholics* for a step-by-step breakdown of the larger arguments (Servant Books, 2014, pp. 45–69).

97 Council of Trent, Session VI.

98 See CCC 1856, 1992, 2020.

99 Or, as some theologians say, freely not rejected. The late Fr. William Most explains how human freedom is preserved even as God's grace acts sovereign upon the soul that is justified in *Catholic Apologetics Today* (Charlotte: TAN Books, 1986), pp. 106–127. See also Reginald Garigou-Lagrange, O.P., *Predestination* (Charlotte: TAN Books, 1998).

100 See 1 Corinthians 6:11; 2 Corinthians 4:16; Ephesians 4:21–25; 1Thessalonians 4:1–3, 5:23; Hebrews 2:11, 10:10, 14, 12:2, 13:14.

101 Council of Trent, Session VI.

102 See Romans 4:5, 6:1–12; 1 Peter 2:24; 2 Corinthians 5:12; Philippians 3:9,

103 Calvary Chapel, a large and growing "non-denominational" Protestant denomination, encourages people to have faith in Christ, repent of their sins, and sincerely pray the Sinner's Prayer. "If you have prayed this, YOU ARE SAVED! You are now completely forgiven, a new creation, innocent in the eyes of God. Welcome to the family of God!" It's just that easy! (http://www.calvarychapelgrangeville.com/how-to-be-born-again, emphasis in original).

104 For a detailed explanation of this doctrine, see J. Michael Miller, C.S.B., *The Shepherd and the Rock* (Huntington, IN: Our Sunday Visitor, 1995), pp. 188–216, and Patrick Madrid, *Pope Fiction: Answers to 30 Myths and Misconceptions about the Papacy* (San Diego: Basilica Press, 1999), pp. 130–162.

105 In my book, *Pope Fiction*, I provide examples from papal history of popes who have come close, but never all the way, to formally teaching error.

106 For details on how to debunk the bogus claim that in Greek, *petros* and *petra* in Matthew 16 mean two different things, see *Pope Fiction*, pp. 37–50.

107 Patrick Madrid, *Why Be Catholic? Ten Answers to a Very Important Question* (New York: Doubleday-Image, 2014), pp. 118–119.

108 See 2 Maccabees 12:43–45; Luke 16:19–31; 1 Corinthians 11:27–32; Hebrews 11:13–16, 32–40; 1 Peter 3:18–19; 4:6; and CCC 1030–1032, 1472–1477.

109 Vainglory is a subtle yet real danger in apologetics. I discuss it at length in my book *Search and Rescue: How to Bring Your Family and Friends into (or Back into) the Catholic Church* (Manchester: Sophia Institute Press, 2000), pp. 21–34, and *On a Mission: Lessons from St. Francis de Sales* (Cincinnati: Servant Books, 2013), pp. 108–112. See also Mark Brumley's warnings about pride in apologetics, *How Not to Share Your Faith: The Seven Deadly Sins of Apologetics and Evangelization* (San Diego: Catholic Answers, 2002), pp. 71–86.

110 "It is … far better to resist this desire [for praise] than to yield to it, for the purer one is from this defilement, the liker is he to God; and, though this vice be not thoroughly eradicated from his heart,—for it does not cease to tempt even the minds of those who are making good progress in virtue,—at any rate, let the desire of glory be surpassed by the love of righteousness, so that, if there be seen anywhere 'lying neglected things which are generally discredited,' if they are good, if they are right, even the love of human praise may blush and yield to the love of truth. For so hostile is this vice to pious faith, if the love of glory be greater in the heart than the fear or love of God, that the Lord said, 'How can you believe, who look for glory from one another, and do not seek the glory which is from God alone?' (John 5:44)" (*City of God*, Book V, ch. 14, in Philip Schaff, trans., *Nicene and Ante-Nicene Fathers* [Peabody, MA: Hendrickson Publishers, Inc., 1995], vol. 2, pp. 96–97).

111 A. G. Sertillanges, O.P., Mary Ryan, trans., *The Intellectual Life: Its Spirits, Conditions, Methods* (Washington, DC: Catholic University of America Press, 1987), p. 142.

112 An echo of this verse is heard in the modern aphorism, "There but for the grace of God go I."

113 "An intentional tendency toward bias" (dictionary.com).

114 Linda Stern provides a helpful guide in *What Every Student Should Know about Avoiding Plagiarism* (New York: Pearson Education, 2006).

115 Note that this is quite different from when you *do* have a good answer, but your opposition refuses to acknowledge it.

116 2 Timothy 3:17.

117 Patrick Madrid, *Envoy for Christ*, p. xv.

118 *The Intellectual Life*, p. 135.

119 NB: Because each of the ten chapters in my book *Why Be Catholic?* covers a different aspect of Catholic apologetics, it is a recommended resource for each of the subsections below.

Glossary of Apologetics Terms

NB: *This is merely a representative list of some of the more common terms encountered in apologetics discussions, especially with Protestants. It is not intended to be exhaustive.*

Absolution: The words of the forgiveness of sins to penitent sinners, in virtue of Christ's gift of the Holy Spirit to the Apostles empowering them to forgive or to retain sins. Administered by a priest or bishop.

Actual Sin: A sin, whether of commission or omission, which is the outcome of a free personal act of the will.

Advent: The liturgical season immediately before Christmas.

Adventism: Generally, the belief that the final return of Christ at the end of the world is near. More specifically, it is associated with particular groups, such as Seventh Day Adventists, who emphasize the imminent return of Christ.

Annihilationism: The belief that the souls of all (or most) human beings will be annihilated or extinguished by God at the conclusion of this mortal life. Some, such as Jehovah's Witnesses, claim that some people will be "resurrected" with new souls and new bodies for eternity, though it is conditional upon their behavior during this life.

Apologetics: The process of presenting, whether formally or informally, a reasoned defense of a belief in response to a denial, challenge, or criticism. The three main categories of apologetics are: natural, Christian, and Catholic.

Apostasy: "The total repudiation of the Christian faith" (CCC 2089) by a baptized Christian, often entailing an explicit denial of the divinity of Christ (e.g., abandoning Christianity for Judaism, Islam, Jehovah's Witnesses, etc.).

Atheism: A lack of belief in any gods and any supernatural realm (e.g., heaven and hell). The atheist worldview is commonly asserted on the basis of naturalism, that is, the belief that the only things that exist are material (i.e., natural) and thus, nothing *supernatural* can exist: neither God nor gods, angels, human souls, heaven, hell, etc.

Atonement: The Catholic doctrine that, by his Incarnation, "justification has been merited for us by the Passion of Christ who offered himself on the cross as a living victim, holy and pleasing to God, and whose blood has become the instrument of atonement for the sins of all men" (CCC 1992). Through Christ's atoning sacrifice, we can be reconciled with God, justified and sanctified in a right relationship with him through grace and the obedience of faith (Romans 1:5).

Baptism: The first and foundational sacrament of the Catholic Church, which both symbolizes and accomplishes cleansing and the eradication of all sin (original and actual), the infusion of sanctifying grace into the soul, and the rebirth and new life that makes us adopted children of God. Baptism is the sacramental "doorway" into the Church Christ established, when water is poured over the head of the one baptized (or he or she is immersed in water) and the baptismal formula is pronounced audibly by the minister: "I baptize you in the name of the Father and of the Son and of the Holy Spirit."

Blasphemy: Speech, thought, or action manifesting contempt for God.

Capital sins: Major sins from which all other sins proceed: "Pride, avarice, envy, wrath, lust, gluttony, and sloth or acedia" (CCC 1866).

Clergy: Those men who receive the sacrament of Holy Orders. "Holy Orders is the sacrament through which the mission entrusted by Christ to his apostles continues to be exercised in the Church until the end of time: thus it is the sacrament of apostolic ministry. It includes three degrees: episcopate, presbyterate, and diaconate" (CCC 1536).

Common Grace: A Protestant concept referring to the grace of God that is either common to all humankind or common to everyone within a particular influence.

Communion: Has various meanings depending on the context. The "communion of saints" refers to the mutual sharing of baptized Christians in the bond of grace and membership in the Body of Christ (see 1 Corinthians 12), as well as sharing holy things. "Holy Communion" refers to the Eucharistic bread and wine, in which Jesus Christ is truly, substantially, and sacramentally present (i.e., "Body, Blood, Soul, and Divinity") under the outward appearances of said Eucharistic elements. Catholics "receive Communion" when they consume the Holy Eucharist, usually at Mass. "Communion" also refers to the bond of unity that exists between the faithful, religious, and clergy of a given diocese and their bishop, as well as with the pope.

Confession: The Catholic sacrament of repentance, forgiveness, and reconciliation. "It is called the *sacrament of confession*, since the disclosure or confession of sins to a priest is an essential element of this sacrament. In a profound sense it is also a 'confession' — acknowledgment and praise — of the holiness of God and of his mercy toward sinful man.

"It is called the *sacrament of forgiveness*, since by the priest's sacramental absolution God grants the penitent 'pardon and peace.'

"It is called the *sacrament of Reconciliation*, because it imparts to the sinner the love of God who reconciles: 'Be reconciled to God.' He who lives by God's merciful love is ready to respond to the Lord's call: 'Go; first be reconciled to your brother.'" (CCC 1424)

Consecration: The formula of words by which the Eucharistic bread and wine in the Mass are transubstantiated by the priest into the Body, Blood, Soul, and Divinity of Jesus Christ.

Consubstantiation: The Lutheran belief that, during a Lutheran communion service, the bread does not change in substance into the Body and Blood of Jesus, though his presence is alongside, or "with," the substance of the bread.

Contrition: The sorrow for sins one has committed, with the intention of sinning no more. Perfect contrition entails sorrow for sin out of love for God, and imperfect contrition (a.k.a. attrition) is sorrow for sin out of fear of punishment.

Creation: The creation of the universe by God's sovereign will and decree, in which he caused the cosmos to come into existence out of nothing, i.e., *ex nihilo.*

Creationism: The view that the biblical account of creation in Genesis 1 and 2 should be understood literally, such that God's bringing the created order into existence spanned a literal seven, twenty-four-hour days (sidereal time). It also commonly entails the rejection of evolution and an assertion of a "young earth" view of creation.

Deacons: The lowest level of the sacrament of Holy Orders; below the rank of priest (presbyter). A "transitional" deacon is a man who is preparing eventually to be ordained a priest. A "permanent" deacon for life, often a married man, is not advanced to the priesthood and may not remarry if his wife should die.

Depravity: Generally refers to man's fallen, sinful nature and estrangement from God due to original sin. Specifically, it is closely associated with John Calvin's reformed theology, denoting the alleged utter, or radical, corruption of the human person as a consequence of original sin. The Catholic Church rejects the notion of "total depravity," in the Calvinist sense.

Dogma: A divinely revealed truth of doctrine that has been formally and explicitly defined by an ecumenical council or a pope. The Real Presence of Christ in the Holy Eucharist, the divinity of Christ, and baptismal regeneration are dogmas; the rosary, calling priests "father," and blessing oneself with holy water are customs and practices, not dogmas.

Dualism: An erroneous philosophical system that holds that spirit and matter are not merely distinct, but are opposed, insofar as matter is "evil" and spirit is good.

Eisegesis: The process of a reader imposing his or her own interpretation into a text in a way that violates the true meaning of that text.

Empiricism: The concept that human beings gain knowledge of things through the medium of our corporeal sense organs — i.e., sight, smell, hearing, taste, touch.

Epistemology: The branch of philosophy that studies knowledge as such and the processes in which human beings gain knowledge.

Eucharist: The Body, Blood, Soul, and Divinity of Jesus Christ, which are truly, substantially, and really present under the forms of bread and wine when confected at Mass.

Excommunication: An ecclesiastical censure. "Certain particularly grave sins incur excommunication, the most severe ecclesiastical penalty, which impedes the reception of the sacraments and the exercise of certain ecclesiastical acts, and for which absolution consequently cannot be granted, according to canon law, except by the Pope, the bishop of the place or priests authorized by them. In danger of death any priest, even if deprived of faculties for hearing confessions, can absolve from every sin and excommunication" (CCC 1463).

Exegesis: The study, explanation, and interpretation of a written text, especially the Bible.

Exorcism: "The act of driving out, or warding off, demons, or evil spirits, from persons, places, or things, which are believed to be possessed or infested by them, or are liable to become victims or instruments of their malice; the means employed for this purpose, especially the solemn and authoritative adjuration of the demon, in the name of God, or any of the higher power in which he is subject" (*Catholic Encyclopedia*).

Fall, the: The profound loss of numerous physical and spiritual gifts that Adam and Eve enjoyed in the Garden of Eden, resulting from their decision to disobey God (see Genesis 3).

Fatalism: The belief that all events are predetermined and inevitable.

Fideism: "A philosophical term meaning a system of philosophy or an attitude of mind, which, denying the power of unaided human reason to reach certitude, affirms that the fundamental act of human knowledge consists in an act of faith, and the supreme criterion of certitude is authority" (*Catholic Encyclopedia*).

Free Will: The innate personal freedom that God bestows on each human being by which he or she can will or reject an object or goal. "The human person participates in the light and power of the divine Spirit. By his reason, he is capable of understanding the order of things established by the Creator. By free will, he is capable of directing himself toward his true good. He finds his perfection "in seeking and loving what is true and good.... Freedom is the power, rooted in reason and will, to act or not to act, to do this or that, and so to perform deliberate actions on one's own responsibility. By free will one shapes one's own life. Human freedom is a force for growth and maturity in truth and goodness; it attains its perfection when directed toward God, our beatitude" (CCC 1704, 1731).

Gnosticism: "A collective name for a large number of greatly varying and pantheistic-idealistic sects, which flourished from some time before the Christian Era down to the fifth century, and which, while borrowing the phraseology and some of the tenets of the chief religions of the day, and especially of Christianity, held matter to be a deterioration of spirit, and the whole universe a depravation of the Deity, and taught the ultimate end of all being to be the overcoming of the grossness of matter and the return to the Parent-Spirit, which return they held to be inaugurated and facilitated by the appearance of some God-sent Savior" (*Catholic Encyclopedia*).

God: The Supreme Being. The one, true, and living creator of heaven and earth and everything, besides himself, that exists. Infinitely unlimited in his perfections (e.g., existence, truth, goodness, beauty, unity, power, knowledge, love, etc.), God is the source of all being. He is Triune: One God in three divine persons — Father, Son, and Holy Spirit.

Grace, Actual: God's interventions, at the time of conversion or in the course of the work of sanctification; the transient movement of grace that gives help to a person in a specific, concrete situation. The supernatural assistance of God bestowed upon a rational being. "Actual grace derives its name, actual, from the Latin *actualis* (*ad actum*), for it is granted by God for the performance of salutary acts and is present and disappears with the action itself" (*Catholic Encyclopedia*).

Grace, Sanctifying: The inner life of God that, when bestowed on a human being, inheres in the soul. It is "an habitual gift, a stable and supernatural disposition that perfects the soul itself to enable it to live with God, to act by his love. Habitual grace, the permanent disposition to live and act in keeping with God's call, is distinguished from actual graces which refer to God's interventions, whether at the beginning of conversion or in the course of the work of sanctification … the gratuitous gift of his life that God makes to us; it is infused by the Holy Spirit into the soul to heal it of sin and to sanctify it…. Sanctifying grace makes us 'pleasing to God.' Charisms, special graces of the Holy Spirit, are oriented to sanctifying grace and are intended for the common good of the Church. God also acts through many actual graces, to be distinguished from habitual grace which is permanent in us" (CCC 2000, 2023, 2024).

Heaven: The dwelling place of God and the angels, and ultimately where the redeemed receive their eternal reward. "The ultimate end and fulfilment of the deepest human longings, the state of supreme, definitive happiness" (CCC 1024).

Hell: The place or state of eternal damnation reserved for the devil and his (fallen) angels and all the souls of the damned. The punishment to which unrepentant sinners who die in the state of serious sin consign themselves for all eternity.

Heresy: "Heresy is the obstinate post-baptismal denial of some truth which must be believed with divine and catholic faith, or it is likewise an obstinate doubt concerning the same" (CCC 2089).

Hermeneutics: The science of the methods of exegesis and biblical interpretation.

Holy Orders: "Holy Orders is the sacrament through which the mission entrusted by Christ to his apostles continues to be exercised in the Church until the end of time: thus it is the sacrament of apostolic ministry. It includes three degrees: episcopate, presbyterate, and diaconate" (CCC 1536).

Holy Spirit: "The proper name of the one whom we adore and glorify with the Father and the Son. The Church has received this name from the Lord and professes it in the Baptism of her new children. The term 'Spirit' translates the Hebrew word *ruah*, which, in its primary sense, means breath, air, wind. Jesus indeed uses the sensory image of the wind to suggest to Nicodemus the transcendent newness of him who is personally God's breath, the divine Spirit. On the other hand, 'Spirit' and 'Holy' are divine attributes common to the three divine persons. By joining the two terms, Scripture, liturgy, and theological language designate the inexpressible person of the Holy Spirit, without any possible equivocation with other uses of the terms 'spirit' and 'holy'" (CCC 691).

Hyperdulia: The special veneration paid to the Blessed Virgin Mary on account of her eminent dignity as Mother of God. It is strictly distinguished from *latria*, the worship and adoration due only to God, but higher than *dulia*, the honor paid to angels and saints.

Hypostatic Union: "A theological term used with reference to the Incarnation to express the revealed truth that in Christ one person subsists in two natures, the Divine and the human. Hypostasis means, literally, that which lies beneath as basis or foundation" (*Catholic Encyclopedia*).

Icon: A painting, carving, imprint, or other sacred image of Jesus Christ, the Blessed Virgin Mary, or another holy personage (saints and angels), venerated with due respect for the persons they represent and used as an aid to devotion, prayer, and liturgy.

Iconoclasm: (i.e., meaning "image breaking" in Greek) the heresy that purports that it is sinful to depict God, angels, and the saints in religious imagery.

Idolatry: The worship of creatures in place of the One True God.

Immaculate Conception: The dogma of Mary's perpetual freedom from all sin, both original and actual, that "from the first moment of her conception the Blessed Virgin Mary was, by the singular grace and privilege of Almighty God, and in view of the merits of Jesus Christ, Savior of mankind, kept free from all stain of original sin" (Bull *Ineffabilis Deus*, 1854).

Immutability: The attribute of God's nature to be unchangeable.

Impeccability: The attribute of an inability to commit sin.

Incarnation: "The mystery and the dogma of the Word made Flesh" (*Catholic Encyclopedia*); that the Second Person of the Blessed Trinity took human nature for our salvation (see John 1:1, 14).

Indulgence: The remission by the Church of the temporal penalty due to forgiven sin, in virtue of the merits of Jesus Christ and the Saints.

Irresistible Grace: Associated with Calvinism, the saving grace applied by God only to a person which He has determined to save.

Jehovah: A modern variant of the Hebrew Tetragrammaton (YHWH) for the name for God, also rendered as "Yahweh."

Jehovah's Witness: The popular name given to the Watch Tower Bible and Tract Society, founded by Charles Taze Russell. Among their many distinct beliefs, the responsibility of its adherents is to study the Bible and to warn as many people as possible about the impending Armageddon "end times" so that they might survive on earth, a "First Judgment," live within Christ's millennial reign on earth, and endure a "Second Judgment."

Justify/Justification: The event or process by which man is made or declared to be righteous in the sight of God. "The grace of the Holy Spirit has the power to justify us, that is, to cleanse us from our sins and to communicate to us 'the righteousness of God through faith in Jesus Christ' and through Baptism.... Through the power of the Holy Spirit we take part in Christ's Passion by dying to sin, and in his Resurrection by being born to a new life; we are members of his Body which is the Church, branches grafted onto the vine which is himself.... The first work of the grace of the Holy Spirit is *conversion*, effecting justification in accordance with Jesus' proclamation at the beginning of the Gospel: 'Repent, for the kingdom of heaven is at hand.' Moved by grace, man turns toward God and away from sin, thus accepting forgiveness and righteousness from on high. 'Justification is not only the remission of sins, but also the sanctification and renewal of the interior man.... Justification *detaches man from sin* which contradicts the love of God, and purifies his heart of sin. Justification follows upon God's merciful initiative of offering forgiveness. It reconciles man with God. It frees from the enslavement to sin, and it heals…. Justification is at the same time *the acceptance of God's righteousness* through faith in Jesus Christ. Righteousness (or 'justice') here means the rectitude of divine love. With justification, faith, hope, and charity are poured into our hearts, and obedience to the divine will is granted us. Justification has been *merited for us by the Passion of Christ* who offered himself on the cross as a living victim, holy and pleasing to God, and whose blood has become the instrument of atonement for the sins of all men. Justification is conferred in baptism, the sacrament of faith. It conforms us to the righteousness of God, who makes us inwardly just by the power of his mercy. Its purpose is the glory of God and of Christ, and the gift of eternal life…. Justification establishes *cooperation between God's grace and man's freedom.* On man's part it is expressed by the assent of faith to the Word of God, which invites him to conversion, and in the cooperation of charity with the prompting of the Holy Spirit who precedes and preserves his assent" (CCC 1987–1993).

Latria: A theological term for that supreme worship and adoration that can be offered to God alone.

Lent: The fast of forty days before Easter.

Liturgy: The Holy Sacrifice of the Mass, primarily. "Originally meant a 'public work' or a 'service in the name of/on behalf of the people.' In Christian tradition it means the participation of the People of God in 'the work of God.' Through the liturgy Christ, our redeemer and high priest, continues the work of our redemption in, with, and through his Church" (CCC 1069).

Logic: The branch of philosophy that deals with evaluating the properties of arguments (e.g., cogency, completeness, validity, soundness, semantics, truth, strength, etc.) and their effectiveness in arriving at truth. There are many different forms of logic including propositional, informal, formal, syllogistic, propositional, modal, etc.

Logos: Word, the Second Person of the Trinity (see John 1:1, 14).

Lord's Supper: The Last Supper; also a term often used by Protestants for their communion services.

Marriage: A natural contract between one man and one woman, which Christ raised to the dignity of a sacrament.

Matrimony (Holy): "A sacrament of the New Law which confers grace for the sanctification of the lawful union of man and woman and for the religious and holy reception and education of offspring. It is a sign of the union of Christ with his Church" (Nicholas Halligan, O.P., *Sacraments of Community Renewal*).

Mediator: "One who brings estranged parties to an amicable agreement. In New Testament theology the term invariably implies that the estranged beings are God and man, and it is appropriated to Christ, the One Mediator. When special friends of God — angels, saints, holy men — plead our cause before God, they mediate 'with Christ'; their mediation is only secondary and is better called intercession" (*Catholic Encyclopedia*).

Merit: "That property of a good work which entitles the doer to receive a reward from him in whose service the work is done.… The word has come to designate also the good work itself, in so far as it deserves a reward from the person in whose service it was performed.

"In the theological sense, a supernatural merit can only be a salutary act, to which God in consequence of his infallible promise owes a supernatural reward, consisting ultimately in eternal life, which is the beatific vision in heaven." (*Catholic Encyclopedia*)

Millennium: The period of one thousand years in which Christ will reign supreme over the world.

Miracle: A sensible event produced by the special intervention of God, transcending the normal order of the universe. "The fundamental idea of millenarianism, as understood by Christian writers, may be set forth as follows: At the end of time Christ will return in all His splendor to gather together the just, to annihilate hostile powers, and to found a glorious kingdom on earth for the enjoyment of the highest spiritual and material blessings; He Himself will reign as its king, and all the just, including the saints recalled to life, will participate in it. At the close of this kingdom the saints will enter heaven with Christ, while the wicked, who have also been resuscitated, will be condemned to eternal damnation. The duration of this glorious reign of Christ and His saints on earth is frequently given as one thousand years. Hence it is commonly known as the 'millennium,' while the belief in the future realization of the kingdom is called 'millenarianism' (or *chiliasm*, from the Greek *chilia*)" (*Catholic Encyclopedia*).

Monogamy: The practice of being married to one woman at a time.

Monotheism: "Monotheism (from the Greek *monos*, 'only', and *theos*, 'god') is a word coined in comparatively modern times to designate belief in the one supreme God, the Creator and Lord of the world, the eternal Spirit, All-powerful, All-wise, and All-good, the Rewarder of good and the Punisher of evil, the Source of our happiness and perfection. It is opposed to Polytheism, which is belief in more gods than one, and to Atheism, which is disbelief in any deity whatsoever. In contrast with Deism, it is the recognition of God's presence and activity in every part of creation. In contrast with Pantheism, it is belief in a God of conscious freedom, distinct from the physical world. Both Deism and Pantheism are religious philosophies rather than religions" (*Catholic Encyclopedia*).

Mormon(ism): The popular name for the Church of Jesus Christ of Latter-day Saints, an American religion founded by Joseph Smith, Jr. (1805–1844), who claimed to be a prophet, seer, and revelator and to have been given "the restored gospel," through a special revelation, including the Book of Mormon.

Mortal Sin (Grave Sin): The most serious category of sin, incurring the loss of sanctifying grace and eternal damnation, unless it is followed by adequate repentance. To fall into this category a sin must be committed with a clear knowledge of its guilt, with full consent of the will, and must concern a grave matter.

Ontological Argument: The argument for God's existence accepting that the concept of God entails the real existence of God.

Original Sin: The sin we inherit by natural descent from Adam, our first father.

Orthodoxy: A religious system of right belief, as contrasted with heresy.

Orthodoxy, Eastern: "The technical name for the body of Christians who use the Byzantine Rite in various languages [e.g., Greek, Ukrainian, Coptic, Russian, etc.] and are in union with the Patriarch of Constantinople" (*Catholic Encyclopedia*) but have (historically) been in schism with the Catholic Church and the pope.

Pantheism: The philosophical system that God and the universe are identical, i.e., that God is the universe and the universe is God.

Panenthism: The view that God (however he/she/it may be defined) is *in* everything. A modern rendering of this view is the *Star Wars* concept of "the Force" — "a binding, metaphysical, and ubiquitous power in the fictional universe of the Star Wars franchise created by George Lucas" (Wikipedia).

Parable: Stories and sayings, well-known proverbs, metaphors, and elaborate allegories commonly used by Jesus as a teaching tool in his public ministry.

Paraclete: From the Greek word παράκλητος (*parácletos*), meaning a helper or advocate, it is a New Testament word for the Holy Spirit.

Pascal's Wager: The argument that it is best to behave as if God exists than to suffer the punishment of hell in the event that God is real. That is, the "smart money" should wager that God does exist, for if you bet that he doesn't exist and you're wrong (i.e., he does exist), you lose everything. And if you bet that he does exist and he doesn't, you lose nothing. But if you bet that he does exist and you win (i.e., he does exist), you win everything.

Patrology: The study of the life and times, writings, and teachings of the early Church Fathers.

Pelagianism: Named after Pelagius, its initial expositor, it is a fifth-century heresy "which denied original sin as well as Christian grace" (*Catholic Encyclopedia*).

Perspicuity: Generally, a meaning clearly expressed, especially in writing. More specifically, it is a commonly accepted view among most Protestants that Scripture is sufficiently clear and its meaning is reasonably obvious. The Calvinist Westminster Confession of Faith says: "All things in Scripture are not alike plain in themselves, nor alike clear unto all, yet those things which are necessary to be known, believed, and observed for salvation are so clearly propounded, and opened in some place of Scripture or other, that not only the learned, but the unlearned, in a due use of the ordinary means, may attain unto a sufficient understanding of them" (1:7).

Pneumatology: The theological study of the role of the Holy Spirit in the Triune God and in his economic and imminent life.

Pope: The popular name given to the Bishop of Rome.

Predestine/Predestination: The divine ordination of salvation for some and not others, destined by God from the beginning. "Taken in its widest meaning, is every divine decree by which God, owing to his infallible prescience of the future, has appointed and ordained from eternity all events occurring in time, especially those which directly proceed from, or at least are influenced by, man's free will" (*Catholic Encyclopedia*).

Prevenient Grace: The grace of God which precedes our human response to that grace. It is a grace, external to the soul, that "nudges" us toward the true and the good, analogous to how a tugboat nudges an ocean liner toward the open sea (cf. John 6:44; Romans 2:4).

Purgatory: A temporary state of purification for those who die in the state of grace and friendship with God (cf. Romans 11:22), but who still have the vestiges of temporal effects due to sin, inordinate attachment to creatures, and whose will is not fully united with God's will. This purification involves suffering (St. Paul uses the analogy of fire to emphasize this), as God's fiery love "burns" away all impurities that may remain. Once this is complete, the soul enters into God's presence, the beatific vision, in which the perfect bliss of beholding Him face to-face lasts forever. (Patrick Madrid, *A Pocket Guide to Purgatory*, OSV, p.11)

Rapture: The main version of the rapture theory is the "pre-tribulation" view, which holds that "the Church" (which is Evangelical and Fundamentalist code for "born-again believers") will be raptured out of this world immediately prior to the Great Tribulation. Adherents of the rapture theory believe this Tribulation will last for seven years. During this time, the Anti-Christ and the Great Beast will arise, and great calamities, persecution, and bloodshed will ensue. At the end of that tribulation period (so the theory goes), Jesus Christ will return to establish a literal 1,000-year kingdom on earth. At the end of that 1,000-year reign, the world will end, he will judge the nations, and then everyone will go either to heaven or hell for all eternity. (Patrick Madrid, *Answer Me This*, OSV, pp. 208–209)

Redemption: Deliverance from sin, suffering, and death by Jesus Christ's atoning passion and death.

Regeneration: Spiritual rebirth that is effected in the soul by the sacrament of Baptism validly administered.

Relativism: The belief that knowledge, truth, and morality exist in relation to the context of culture and society and are not absolute.

Repentance: The acknowledgement and condemnation of one's own sins with a conscious turning to God.

Revelation: The body of truth about God that He discloses to mankind.

Ritual: The prescribed form of words of a liturgical function.

Rosary: A form of prayer in which five decades of Hail Marys are recited, each decade preceded by the Lord's Prayer and followed by the Gloria Patri; counted on a string of beads or a ring.

Sacrament: The means by which Christians partake in the "mystery of Christ"; an outward and visible sign of a real and inward grace.

Sacred Tradition: The living, ongoing transmission of the Deposit of Faith from generation to generation in the life of the Church. It is comprised of two components, written and oral, which are also two united and complimentary yet distinct modes of transmission of the one gospel of Jesus Christ: Scripture and unwritten Apostolic Tradition (see 1 Corinthians 11:2; 2 Thessalonians 2:15). Sacred Tradition conveys not merely the objective data of Divine Revelation, but also its authentic *meaning* (see Patrick Madrid, *Scripture and Tradition in the Church*, Sophia Institute Press, 2014).

Sacrifice: The offering of the suffering or death of one (typically living creature) to make atonement for the sins of others.

Sanctifying Grace: The permanent disposition that perfects the soul to enable it to live in communion with God and to act by his love; a grace that must be maintained.

Semi-Pelagianism: The heresy that purports that humans can achieve salvific grace under their own power, without God's grace, and can retain that status without God's help, or further grace.

Sin: Any thought, word, or deed willfully committed as an offense against God. "Sins are rightly evaluated according to their gravity. The distinction between mortal and venial sin,…

"*Mortal sin* destroys charity in the heart of man by a grave violation of God's law; it turns man away from God, who is his ultimate end and his beatitude, by preferring an inferior good to him.

"*Venial sin* allows charity to subsist, even though it offends and wounds it.

"Mortal sin, by attacking the vital principle within us — that is, charity — necessitates a new initiative of God's mercy and a conversion of heart which is normally accomplished within the setting of the sacrament of reconciliation." (CCC 1854–1856)

Sola Fide: Latin for [justification] by faith alone. It is the Protestant notion that God's pardoning for guilty sinners is granted through faith alone, excluding all works, unto the end of salvation. Forensic and extrinsic to the soul of the person justified, the Lutheran Augsburg Confession describes *sola fide* as, "men cannot be justified before God by their own strength, merits, or works, but are freely justified for Christ's sake, through faith, when they believe that they are received into favor, and that their sins are forgiven for Christ's sake, who, by His death, has made satisfaction for our sins. This faith God imputes for righteousness in His sight."

Sola Scriptura: The Protestant principle that the Bible is the sole, infallible, formally sufficient, supreme authority in all matters of Christian doctrine. Most highly systemized in the Reformed branch of Protestantism, the principle is expressed in the Westminster Confession of Faith thus: "The whole counsel of God concerning all things necessary for His own glory, man's salvation, faith and life, is either expressly set down in Scripture, or by good and necessary consequence may be deduced from Scripture: unto which nothing at any time is to be added, whether by new revelations of the Spirit, or traditions of men" (I:6).

Soul: The immaterial principle of life and intelligence, giving living things motion from within. Human souls are immortal, utterly simple (i.e., does not have parts or divisions), and eternal.

Sufficiency, formal and material: Protestants generally espouse some form of the alleged "sufficiency of the Bible" with greater or lesser degrees of rigor. Most Baptists, Evangelical Lutherans, Calvinists, and non-denominational Evangelicals believe that the Bible is not just materially sufficient (i.e., it contains all necessary teachings for the Church, though some are only implicit at best), but *formally* sufficient, in that it requires no outside authority (e.g., popes, church, councils, etc.) to adequately and accurately interpret its meaning (see the Westminster Confession of Faith for a full exposition of this view).

Syllogism: A three-part form of an argument that reasons from two premises to a conclusion; e.g., "If all As are also Bs, and all Bs are also Cs, then it follows that all As are Cs."

Teleology: The science of ends or final causes, especially important for apologetics with regard to moral issues.

Theism: A philosophical worldview that posits the existence of a transcendent, personal God who created, preserves, and governs the universe.

Theology: The study of God and divine revelation.

Total Depravity: "Probably the most misunderstood tenet of Calvinism. When Calvinists speak of humans as 'totally depraved,' they are making an extensive, rather than an intensive, statement. The effect of the fall upon man is that sin has extended to every part of his personality — his thinking, his emotions, and his will. Not necessarily that he is intensely sinful, but that sin has extended to his entire being.

"The unregenerate (unsaved) man is dead in his sins (Romans 5:12). Without the power of the Holy Spirit, the natural man is blind and deaf to the message of the gospel (Mark 4:11). This is why Total Depravity has also been called 'Total Inability.' The man without a knowledge of God will never come to this knowledge without God's making him alive through Christ (Ephesians 2:1-5)." (reformed.org/calvinism)

Transubstantiation: The conversion of the whole substance of the Communion bread and wine into the whole substance of the Body and Blood of Christ, with only the accidents (i.e., the appearances of the bread and wine) remaining.

Trinity: The mystery that God is numerically and individually one, existing in three Persons; that the Divine essence exists identically in three Persons really distinct from each other.

Type, Typology: Commonly associated with biblical theology and Bible based apologetics, a person, place, or thing that, in the Old Testament, foreshadows or prefigures something or someone in the New Testament, usually Jesus Christ. Paul's letter to the Hebrews, for example, is rich in typological examples.

Universalism: The doctrine that hell is purgative and, therefore, temporary willing all intelligent beings in the end to be saved.

About the Author

PATRICK MADRID is a life-long Catholic. He hosts the popular daily *Patrick Madrid Show* on Immaculate Heart Radio (Monday to Friday, 6 to 9 a.m., Pacific Time). And before launching that show, he hosted the *Right Here, Right Now* show, broadcast on approximately three hundred AM and FM radio stations across the United States as well as on Sirius Satellite Radio and globally via shortwave. He is also a frequent guest and occasional guest-host on the *Catholic Answers Live* radio program.

Patrick has authored or edited twenty-four books on Catholic themes, including *Life Lessons, Why Be Catholic?, Search and Rescue, Does the Bible Really Say That?*, and the acclaimed *Surprised by Truth* series.

Commenting publicly on the effectiveness of Patrick's approach to doing apologetics, Cardinal Edward Egan, Archbishop Emeritus of New York, said, "How do you bring a friend or relative back into the Church? First you pray. Then, you follow Patrick Madrid's advice in [his book] *Search and Rescue*."

Patrick worked at Catholic Answers for eight years, where he served as vice president. A veteran of a dozen formal, public debates with Protestant ministers, Mormon leaders, and other non-Catholic spokesmen, Patrick has presented countless seminars on Catholic themes, in English and Spanish, at parishes, universities, and conferences across the United States and around the world.

For nearly thirty years, Patrick has published numerous popular articles on Scripture, Church history, patristics, apologetics, and evangelization in various Catholic and

Protestant periodicals, and he has contributed scholarly articles on apologetics to the *New Catholic Encyclopedia*.

He earned a Bachelor of Science degree in business at the University of Phoenix, as well as a B.Phil. in philosophy and an M.A. in dogmatic theology at the Pontifical College Josephinum (Columbus, Ohio). He is currently pursuing a doctorate in Church history.

Patrick has served as an adjunct professor of theology at Franciscan University of Steubenville and currently teaches as an adjunct professor of theology in the graduate theology program at Holy Apostles College and Seminary in Cromwell, Connecticut.

Married for thirty-five years, Patrick and his wife Nancy have been blessed by the Lord with eleven children and eighteen grandchildren (so far). His website is www.patrickmadrid.com.